MW01427798

Backyard Homestead

The Ultimate Homesteading Guide to Growing Your Own Food, Raising Chickens, and Mini-Farming for Self Sufficiency and Profit

© Copyright 2020

The contents of this book may not be reproduced, duplicated, or transmitted without direct written permission from the author.

Under no circumstances will any legal responsibility or blame be held against the publisher for any reparation, damages, or monetary loss due to the information herein, either directly or indirectly.

Legal Notice:

This book is copyright protected. This is only for personal use. You cannot amend, distribute, sell, use, quote, or paraphrase any part of the content within this book without the consent of the author.

Disclaimer Notice:

Please note the information within this document is for educational and entertainment purposes only. Every attempt has been made to provide accurate, up to date, and reliable information. No warranties of any kind are expressed or implied. Readers acknowledge that the author is not engaging in the rendering of legal, financial, medical, or professional advice. The content of this book has been derived from various sources. Please consult a licensed professional before attempting any techniques outlined in this book.

By reading this document, the reader agrees that under no circumstances are is the author responsible for any losses, direct or indirect, which are incurred because of the use of information within this document, including, but not limited to, —errors, omissions, or inaccuracies.

The information herein is offered for informational purposes solely and is universal as so. The presentation of the information is without contract or any guarantee assurance.

The trademarks used are with no consent, and the publication of the trademark is without permission or backing by the trademark owner. All trademarks and brands within this book are for clarifying purposes only and are owned by the owners themselves, not affiliated with this document.

Contents

INTRODUCTION 1
CHAPTER 1: REASONS FOR STARTING A HOMESTEAD 2
CHAPTER 2: SIX TOP THINGS TO CONSIDER WHEN PLANNING A HOMESTEAD 10
CHAPTER 3: MAKING A PLAN FOR YOUR MINI FARM 19
   SAMPLE BACKYARD HOMESTEAD LAYOUTS 22
CHAPTER 4: SELECTING YOUR SEED STOCK AND CULTIVARS 27
CHAPTER 5: HOW TO SELECT CHICKENS AND BUILD A COOP 35
   SELECTING THE RIGHT CHICKENS FOR YOUR HOMESTEAD 35
   HERITAGE BREEDS 36
   ALTERNATIVE BREEDS 37
   RAISING CHICKENS FOR SLAUGHTER 39
   SILKIES AND BRAHMAS – MOMMA HENS 41
   OTHER FACTORS TO CONSIDER WHEN RAISING CHICKENS 42
CHAPTER 6: PREPARING YOUR KITCHEN FOR A HOMESTEAD 46
   CHECKLIST OF SUPPLIES 47
   HOMESTEADING TOOLS AND SUPPLIES FOR YOUR KITCHEN 49
   SPECIALTY KITCHEN TOOLS FOR A HOMESTEAD 50
   HOW TO GET AND STAY ORGANIZED 51

CHAPTER 7: HARVESTING AND PRESERVING THE FRUITS OF YOUR LABOR 55
   Root Cellars – What You Need to Know 59
CHAPTER 8: MAKING A PROFIT FROM YOUR HOMESTEAD 62
CHAPTER 9: 8 RESOURCES TO CONSIDER 72
CHAPTER 10: CARE AND MAINTENANCE 79
   Caring for Gardens 79
   How to Make Your Homestead as Low Maintenance as Possible 84
CHAPTER 11: SHARING YOUR LEARNING EXPERIENCE 88
   Vlogs 88
   Blogs 91
CHAPTER 12: EXPANDING YOUR HOMESTEAD 98
CONCLUSION 102
RESOURCES 103

Introduction

Backyard Homestead introduces the principles of homesteading with hands-on methods that beginners can use right away. This complete guide walks you through all the great reasons to homestead, how to get started, what challenges you should plan for, and much more.

Don't miss the opportunity to learn about homesteading in an easy to understand and practical manner. These methods are fool-proof and have been used by households operating in a self-sufficient manner for decades or even centuries. Many people now remember that only a few generations ago most households relied on their own garden, raised chickens, and engaged within their community. This self-sufficiency is once again becoming a more normal situation. It doesn't matter if you have a small backyard or acres of property, you can get started with the basics and learn how to plan and develop your homestead as your skills develop even further.

Keep reading to discover how you can implement modern techniques to master age-old methods of cultivating your land and a lifestyle that fits your values.

Chapter 1: Reasons for Starting a Homestead

It doesn't matter if you've always had an interest in gardening or if changes in the economy and personal security have made you consider going back to homesteading. Anyone can homestead if they have a little property and a touch of patience. Okay, there are certain things you will need, but the most important thing to get you started is your reason you want to do it. With one good reason, you can drastically change the course of day-to-day happenings of your life.

One or more of these reasons may have spurred your interest in homesteading. Exploring the reasons you're interested in homesteading can help you set out your goals and plans before you jump right in.

Better Health

It's generally common knowledge that eating organic fruit and vegetables is better for your health. That belief leads most people to the conclusion that if they grew their own fruit and vegetables, it would be a better option than shopping in stores. There is some truth to homegrown fruit and vegetables having more health benefits, better nutrient density, and fewer additives. However, it's important to take a rational or scientific approach to the association between farming and health.

Let's roll through some quick facts that can help you determine if this is the right reason for you to start homesteading:

- Homegrown food does have more nutrients; vegetables and fruit begin to lose nutritional value within 24 hours of harvest, ergo, fresher food means more nutritional benefits.
- No presence of genetic modification – at this time there is no conclusive evidence that GMOs are harmful. However, they aren't natural and are likely not beneficial.
- No harmful pesticides, waxes, or other chemicals. You have control over unwanted additives to your food.

Along with homegrown fruit and vegetables, you can make better health choices through homesteading by raising chickens, goats, and cattle. Essentially what you're doing regarding your health is taking control over the processes applied to your food before it gets to your table. You don't have to worry about pesticides unless you're choosing which pesticides to use in your garden. Many homesteaders use only natural remedies such as vinegar or "garden buddies" – specific herbs that can drive out pests. This level of control can allow for a much healthier lifestyle.

For example, did you know there are at least twenty-one common fruits and vegetables, including avocados and apples, that are treated with wax before they arrive at grocery stores? When it comes to health, it goes without saying that organic is better. Homegrown is also better, as long as you take measures to ensure that health and safety are your priority.

Educational Experience

How much do you know about the food you buy? Do you know the life cycle of a plant? What about the incubation period for chicken eggs?

Homesteading leads you to ask questions that would never cross your mind. It makes you think about growth and development as a cycle rather than a journey with a destination. Many homesteaders cite the challenge or the educational experience as the reason for starting. Many others report they started homesteading because they had children and wanted to teach them the value of growing their own food and being self-sustaining.

If you're not sure about including the educational experience as part of your plan for making goals, consider the educational gaps that will become present as you start homesteading. Whether you want the education to be part of your experience or not, it will be necessary to have a successful garden and crop rotations. Most of our basic survival and living skills have been lost because of the massive development of our food product supply chain. On the part of economics, it's made tons of jobs and helped build a stable element in our day-to-day society. But when it comes to developing yourself as a person, it's evident that most of us lack the necessary skills to live independently.

Connection with Your Food

It's easy to go through a Jack-in-the-Box drive-through or order out from Slaters 50/50 and forget that your burger once had a face. Now there's nothing terribly wrong about eating meat. However, it is important to understand where your food comes from and what role it plays in your life. Many who include chickens or milking cows or goats in their homesteading plan find that they do connect with the animals. It can make dealing with the loss of an animal, or consumption, difficult to handle at certain times. That deeper connection to food can not only make you more appreciative of the contributions these animals make in our daily lives, but also the role of food waste in society. People who want to connect with their food better may also aspire to lead zero-waste lives or better manage their connection with the Earth and life around us.

Homesteading can drastically change how you view food and food sources, both financially and emotionally. Very few people use this reason as their primary decision-maker to start homesteading. And, of those people, you'll likely encounter more vegetarians or vegans as our modern lifestyles have disconnected us from the correlation between animals and meat.

No matter what your choice of diet, having a deeper connection with your food can change that relationship exponentially. Where you may once have taken for granted the overstocked shelves in a superstore, you suddenly begin to realize the lifecycles and planning that go into raising chickens or managing crop rotations. Even if this isn't your primary reason for homesteading, it's likely to be a byproduct of the homesteading experience.

Better At-Home Dining Experience

At-home dining is something that we can all enjoy. It's highly likely that you and most people you know can cook better food than that you normally experience when dining out. When you look at the most commonly frequented restaurant chains, including Texas Roadhouse and The Cheesecake Factory, most items on their menu are not made in-house. Rather they're prepared in a manufacturing facility, packaged, and then usually steamed-in-a-bag or fried on site.

But having said this, how can homesteading lead to better at-home dining? Three primary factors can affect your cooking and dining experiences at home.

First, fresh tomatoes, eggs, herbs, and everything else always taste better. Food grown or cultivated at home always tastes better. Honestly, it might be entirely psychological if it weren't for the chemicals and treatments that grocery-store food goes through. We've already covered how homegrown food is better. But when it comes to preparing and eating food, there's the matter of freshness. Even if you shop at higher-end markets such as Sprouts or Whole Foods, that produce spends hours or even days on trucks traveling in the open air and under the sun; the food simply can't stay fresh in those conditions. When you're homesteading, the food goes from the vine or plant into your kitchen or refrigerator. You can't get fresher than that!

Second, you have greater control over possible contaminants and your ingredient management. Homesteading can open your eyes. One homesteader explained that she started after learning that about 95% of grocery store products contained corn or corn byproducts. Well, some things such as cornbread mix were understandable, other things such as fruit snacks were not. What's troublesome with revelations like this is that most of the food in our grocery stores is not as nutrient-dense as it should be because of the presence of corn byproducts. It was one of the things that changed her mind about buying from stores, and it's helped others to see the many advantages of homesteading. For many, tidbits of information like this are the first step in the educational experience that comes with deciding to become a homesteader.

Finally, we have a psychological element. You're more likely to take more care in preparing your ingredients when you are the one who put in all the hard work of growing those vegetables or milking that cow. If you nurtured those little tomatoes from sprouts to sun-ripened globes of goodness, you're going to be much more upset if your sauce doesn't turn out well. So, the natural solution is to handle your ingredients well and develop your cooking skills.

Freedom from Corporate Product-Supply Chain

There are many social and economic effects that we experience every day because of the corporate product-supply chain, better known as the U.S. Food System. Now this reason for homesteading isn't exclusively about living off the grid or "fighting the system." Homesteading can be beneficial for your local economy and strengthen you, and your neighbor's, role in the nation's security and stability.

The U.S. Food System has become a series of tournaments where mass-producers compete for space in the most frequented grocery stores across the nation. That's a drastically different picture from what was happening a few decades ago, where farmers contributed to local or regionalized grocery stores. It's extremely difficult for local farmers to rival major agriculture manufacturers, although there is an increased awareness of local farmers and the need to buy locally.

Dependence on the system that feeds into your major grocery stores perpetuates the difficulties that local farmers and local economies experience. The freedom from this structure can allow you to eat seasonally and better manage or simplify your life when it comes to food. When was the last time you saw anything but the general vegetables in your store? You'd be hard-pressed to find rhubarb in most common grocery stores, even when it is in season.

Security from Panic Buying and Compromised Economic Situations

In times of crisis, people rush to the grocery store. The brief history of panic buying includes the 13 days leading up to the Cuban-missile crisis, the 1973 and 1979 oil crises, Y2K, the 2008 economic recession, and of course, 2020's COVID-19. That's six major instances of panic buying in less than 60 years. These examples are limited to survival-style panic buying, meaning that we didn't include the New Coke panic buying or the resurgence of Crystal Pepsi panic buying. Then you have seasonal over-buying of Frankenberry, Count Chocula, Peeps, and other limited-time items.

Aside from panic buying, you have compromised economic situations. There are times when the agriculture or food service industries are compromised by events that don't largely affect other industries. For example, the Mad Cow outbreak in 2003 made prices of beef skyrocket across multiple countries, although the United Kingdom was the most affected. It economically impacted countries that didn't actually have cases of Mad Cow. The agriculture industry doesn't have to experience the full-scale effect of the Dust Bowl all over again to create an economic issue. One bad crop rotation in America, especially a corn crop, can lead to extensive issues mostly inside grocery stores. People aren't losing their jobs or going out and buying tons of toilet paper at a time, but they are facing extreme price hikes because of the scarcity of primary staples of our diet.

When you're homesteading, you don't have to worry about that. If you raise and slaughter your own cattle or chickens, changes in meat prices aren't really an issue. You might be more concerned about the availability of alfalfa. You don't have to worry about panic buying as much when you know that most of your household supplies come from materials that you cultivate. It's possible to use natural ingredients grown at home for a great variety of other household products, including cleaners, skin and body care products, and more. Many people turn to homesteading following a panic-buying experience because it's traumatic. Panic-buying leads to real shortages with a serious impact on the people who didn't go out and panic-buy. The only ones purely unaffected by panic buying are the people who cultivate their own food.

Understand Your Reasons for Homesteading

Your personal reasons for homesteading are probably good reasons, even if they're not listed above. What you have to consider when you start planning, or even just thinking about the possibility of homesteading, is how you'll lay out your goals. Homesteading, especially backyard homesteading, calls for a very specific formula for success. It is made up of two parts planning, one part hard work, and one part consistent maintenance. Your reasons will direct your goals and put you on the path to make a plan that will allow you to execute those goals. It's critical that you clearly understand your reasons for homesteading.

Some reasons that people list for their desire to homestead are actually the products of a homesteading lifestyle. It's like saying, "I want to open a company to earn money." You don't have to own a business to make money, and you don't have to homestead to simplify your life or better control your diet choices. However, those are huge payoffs that come with growing your own food or raising your own chickens. Let's break down why simplification and controlling diet are not reasons for homesteading but instead natural benefits.

Simplifying your life is not an immediate thing you'll experience through homesteading. In fact, you'll largely complicate your life for the first year. You'll worry over plant health, ground rotations, planting methods, and seeding. You'll add numerous daily tasks to your schedule such as watering plants, feeding chickens, gathering eggs, weeding planters or troughs, and more. After your first year, when you have a schedule and know what works, you will probably have a much simpler life. You won't worry about what to get at the grocery store, at least in terms of vegetables. You won't need to worry so much about menu planning, or to dine out as often, and certainly won't have to worry so much over your budget. If you thought that simplifying your life was your reason for homesteading, you might consider prioritizing one of the reasons above to help manage your goals and planning.

Better control over your diet is another direct product of homesteading, but if you're looking to use it as your reason for homesteading, you might reconsider and use better health as your primary reason or goal. Often when people start homesteading to limit or restrict their diet, they give up or are too restrictive. What you plant dictates what you eat, and if you're only planting veggies to restrict your diet, you may create so many restrictions that it's not sustainable for your health. No matter what your reason is for homesteading, sustainability is the foundation of a successful homestead and a healthy diet. If you only grow zucchini and tomato, it's not sustainable. Diversity, nutrition, and the season will greatly impact your homestead planning, and if controlling your diet is your primary reason, you may need to reframe your mindset on your diet in order to match the goal of health, wellness, and home-growing your produce and possibly raising animals.

Your reason for homesteading is largely purposeful to you and will direct how you approach your plan and execution of creating your backyard homestead. In the chapters to follow, you'll see how your reasons for homesteading will play a part in building self-sustainability, plotting out your mini-farm, building coops, preparing your kitchen, and much more. Very few people start out understanding the full impact of homesteading on day-to-day events, and homesteading is an ongoing learning experience even for those who have been at it for years. Take your reason and make it a lifestyle for homesteading success.

Chapter 2: Six Top Things to Consider When Planning a Homestead

When you're working on putting a homestead together, you'll need to break the giant project down into tiny manageable tasks. Planning can drastically change the level of success you experience on your homestead, and you'll need to start planning before you even buy your first seeds. Not only will you learn how to plan out each section of your homestead, but you'll develop planning skills that you'll need to maintain your homestead, share your experiences, and connect with more people through the homesteading community.

So, where should you start? You'll need to decide what elements of homesteading you'll choose to participate in, and then what other elements will naturally come from those choices.

Will you:
- Grow vegetables and roots?
- Grow herbs?
- Plant fruit trees?
- Keep chickens?
- Raise chickens for multiple purposes?

- Keep goats for ground maintenance and milking?
- Raise cattle for the diary?
- Raise cattle for meat or slaughter?
- Preserve food through canning, dehydrating, freezing, or in a root cellar?
- Make your own goods such as jams, preserves, and dairy products?

As you go through each of these ask yourself these questions:
- Do I have the space available?
- Is my climate appropriate?
- What equipment or furnishings will I need?

Understanding your answers to these questions doesn't mean that you can or can't homestead. Virtually anyone can build more sustainability into their households through growing food and upcycling. However, it can drastically change what homesteading means for you. Use this list to set your priorities and understand your current limitations.

To help explore your possibilities and potential limitations, we'll go through the planning element in four parts.

1. Land use
2. Household needs and limits
3. Location restrictions
4. Skills and abilities

Land Use

Remember that the idea of a homestead is for self-sufficient living. You only need to cultivate the land in a way that supports your style of living and a healthy diet. If you're not a big, fruit-that-grows-on-trees kind of person, then focus on berries and vine fruit instead. Each of these things will help feed the other. For example, from the garden, you can grow vegetables to feed the chickens and goats. The goats (with some rotation) will help keep your ground in good condition and create fertilizer for your garden, and they also produce milk. A homestead is truly the place where nothing goes to waste, and what happens when you have actual, "I can't use this," waste? It goes on the compost pile, to create better soil for next year.

Consider how you answered the questions above and how important each factor is to you when it comes to homesteading. If you don't have access to certain resources, then you may need to reprioritize your homestead goals temporarily.

Household Needs and Limits

How much self-sufficiency can you build into your household? With an open mind, a touch of creativity, and some ingenuity, you may be able to restrict or even eliminate your regular shopping habits. Of course, no one judges you for the occasional purchase! But imagine if you could grow all of your vegetables right in your backyard and likely have a much more diverse offering than you can find in your local grocery store? You can have all the eggs you could need for the year with just a few chickens. With a goat or cow, you can have a regular flow of milk. When you expand and bring in rabbits, you have access to some of the more expensive meat varieties without the expensive price tag.

"Happiness belongs to the self-sufficient." – Aristotle

So, knowing that your household could be almost completely self-sufficient, even to the extent of creating your own cleaners and skincare products, the question becomes once again about space and storage.

How and where will you store or hold your goods? Some items can last for years on a shelf, for example, jarred peaches. Those peaches, if jarred properly, are something you can hold onto for a long time. But your tree won't stop producing more peaches, so what will you do with those? Plants produce at their own rate and you can either:

- Eat at the rate of plant production (a tough task unless you have a large family)
- Pickle, jar, can, or store in a controlled environment
- Sell or share your excess

Part of learning how to homestead is learning how to do things the way they were done not so long ago. It does seem archaic to have a root cellar or to spend your Sundays pickling eggs, but honestly, these are the tried and true methods for preservation. But what if you genuinely don't have space to store everything properly? Just because something can be jarred or canned doesn't mean that you can continue storing the new influx for weeks or months at a time.

The good news is that homesteading allows you to share the wealth because, for most residences trying to sustain a household, there's always excess. If you genuinely run out of space to store your harvest, any part of it, then share. Sell fresh items at a local farmer's market or give away items to your neighbors and friends. It's a great way to become friendlier with neighbors, and a dozen eggs can earn a lot of forgiveness for the strife over your chicken's noise level.

We've managed to cover how you can be entirely self-sufficient and that if you run into storage space limitations, you have other options. But what about your access to equipment and supplies or even the financial means to get started? Many people enjoy saying, "I can't," but they don't look at the situation enough to generate any creative solutions. Yes, you may need pallets, wood, saws (which are expensive), seeds (which can become expensive), and help in the way of manual labor. However, there are excellent solutions to all of these challenges. If you're facing some trouble over these challenges to getting started, here are a few creative and often low-budget solutions:

- Pallets are an excellent wood source and can often be purchased from trucking yards for less than $3 per pallet.
- Start with cheaper crops – you don't need a rare breed of cucumber; you just need cucumbers.
- Rent equipment from hardware stores
- Borrow equipment from friends or family (and if you want to, call them in to help!)

Homesteading is hard, and one of the most difficult things that people experience is the new sensation of replacing, "I can't" with "I'll figure it out." However, it is a very empowering mindset change. Nothing is stopping you except space limitations, and when you hit those limitations, you can share or sell your goods until you re-stabilize your goods rotation and have space again.

Location and Financial Restrictions

Location and financial restrictions do pose some unique challenges, and it's difficult to overcome these issues sometimes. When it comes to location, your city or county may have restrictions on noise levels, the number of animals you can have on a property, or where you can dig or move utilities throughout your property. Additionally, if you're renting your home, you may feel like you're even more restricted.

Let's cover the issues with the local government first. The biggest trouble is running water and power through your yard. Usually, water isn't an issue because you will be creating nothing more complex than you would expect with a sprinkler system, and many households have those across the country. But electricity is a big obstacle. If you need to connect a water heater and lights out in your chicken coop but need to run a line to make that happen, you may need certain permits from your city. They don't want you to create a fire hazard or not adhere to local electrical or building codes, and they don't want you accidentally digging into an already existing utility line. These are pretty reasonable concerns, so if you need to move access to electricity, talk to your city or county office about your property and your options. Know that extension cords are not a long-term solution, and they can be dangerous, especially if you have animals such as chickens or goats that can get to them and fray the wires.

Now, if you're renting, you likely do have some restrictions. However, you can create collapsible structures. For example, most property owners aren't opposed to garden planters, hanging gardens, or trough gardens as long as they don't do lasting damage to the yard. And you might choose to use hydroponics in your garage, or similar alternatives to avoid disrupting the yard. Renting is complicated and varies from person to person. If you're renting now, you might consider making it a priority to put some money aside to purchase land or participate in a local community garden where you can still garden in the dirt and reap the benefits. Finally, you might explore the options for loans or grants that help small farms and homesteads get started. You can find more resources on funding options in Chapter Nine.

Then there are animal zoning regulations that apply to both homeowners and renters. These regulations vary from county to county and often have nothing to do with the noise levels, but the space and the humane raising of animals. A general guide, although your area may vary, gives a limit of two cattle, four sheep or goats, or two pigs on a 1/2-acre property. These guidelines typically use an "or", not an "and", clause meaning that you can have two cattle or two pigs but not both. There are also restrictions on the total volume of animals, and specific restrictions on how many chickens, dogs, and even cats or rabbits you can keep. You can find your local regulations by searching online "animal zoning regulations + (name of your county)" or visiting your county regulations office.

These challenges bring us back to the notion that some planning and prioritizing can help you overcome many obstacles. But, with location and financial obstacles, there may be some things you have to accept. If your city restricts noise levels and doesn't allow residential chickens, then you may not be able to keep chickens given your current residence. Animal zoning regulations are a struggle. Here are some creative options to overcome or work around common obstacles with location and financial limitations:

• Segment your homestead in a way that fits your budget. For example, build a chicken coop with your savings in January, then build trough gardens with your tax return in April. In May, purchase your seeds, then in July buy your fruit trees, and in September set up your goat pen.

• There are resources for funding (grants and loans) available through the government on a federal level, state level, and depending on your location, possibly even through your county or city offices.

• If you can't garden at home, get involved with a community garden, or help to set one up near your neighborhood.

- Prioritize your animals or use a smaller blend to adhere to animal zoning – for example, having one goat, one cow, and four chickens may be doable versus having two cows and 10 chickens. Explore different ways to stay within local regulations by prioritizing your short and long-term homesteading goals.
- Problems with running electrical underground: consult with a local electrician to determine if you can weather/child/animal protect a wall-mounted electrical line.

Skills and Abilities

You know that with some creative planning, you can get around most limitations, but what about the things you just don't know how to do? Well, homesteading is an ongoing learning process. Even after you've run a homestead for five or even ten years, you'll learn new things. During the first three years of homesteading, however, you'll face a steep learning curve. Fortunately, if you don't learn something the first time, it doesn't mean that your entire mini farm fails.

You may need to learn how to build things with your hands, such as planter boxes or a chicken coop. You will need to learn how to care for and maintain plants, and maybe some small animals. However, you may not have realized you must also learn how to plan around weather changes, and even develop your decision-making skills. Imagine that a heatwave blows through your town, and your poor chickens and rabbits have no relief but the natural shade, which is hardly any relief at all. Do you spray them down with water? Do you freeze water bottles and let them huddle around the sweet icy relief? You will build skills and abilities as you go, but to get started, you'll want to learn about gardening best practices and basic building skills. You might also want to hone your skills on upcycling, as it gets the creative homesteader juices flowing.

How to Set Realistic Goals for Your Homestead Plan

Nothing is more motivating than a worthy goal, and with homesteading, you need to think both long-term and short-term. Your goals will help guide you as you build your homestead and develop it over the first few years. Here are a few common sample goals for new homesteaders. Use them to help get you thinking about your goals!

Long-Term Goals
- Purchase a lot for a large homestead – 10 years + goal
- Add steers to cow herd – 5-year goal
- Raise rabbits for meat – 3-year goal
- Raise chickens – 1-year goal

Short-Term Goals
- Plan seasonal garden and crop rotations on a calendar – 1-week goal
- Build three box gardens – 1-month goal
- Plant first seasonal garden – 2-month goal
- Obtain all materials necessary to build a chicken coop and "run" – 3-month goal
- Make space for a dairy cow – 4-month goal
- Start preserving first harvest – 4-month goal
- Purchase dairy cow – 5-month goal
- Remove eggs from your shopping list – 6-month goal

Prioritizing your Goals

Always prioritize what is most important to you. Some things are easier to manage at different times of the year, so consider that. But in addition to your listed goals, you might create a list of skills you need to help set your priorities. Using the short-term goal list above as an example, the first goal was to plan out the season's crops on a calendar. That means you would take time researching when certain plants thrive. The second goal is building planters, and you might do that research at the same time as when you're planning your calendar because many of the resources may be the same.

When you're planning your homestead, it might seem like every big milestone is weeks or months away. But with a map of your yard, after you've planned out the layout, you can start looking for things to do right now. You might prepare your yard, buy the lumber, or get a feel for the airflow and sun-to-shade ratio on your property. There's always something to be done on a homestead, and you can start right now as long as you have a basic plan.

Chapter 3: Making a Plan for Your Mini Farm

When you're planning out your homestead, you'll quickly become a master project manager, goal setter, and resource navigator. Possibly the most difficult part of homesteading is the initial planning. As Brett Brian famously said, "Farming is a profession of hope," and all the planning that you're doing right now is laying down your seeds of hope.

Setting Realistic Goals as You Plan

As you go through the planning, you'll want to keep realistic goal setting in mind. That doesn't mean lowering your expectations. It simply means that your goals are within the realms of reason. Agriculture and homesteading works largely on natural laws and a strong reliance on Mother Nature. If you plant seeds today, you certainly can't eat tomatoes tomorrow. Setting realistic goals means including the average period of time required for any given activity or development and ensuring that the goal is measurable. Here are two examples of a good goal and a less than realistic goal:

Unrealistic Goal: Make planter boxes and plant seeds.

Realistic goal: Buy materials and make planter boxes this weekend, set up mulch and water systems for seeding next weekend.

The second goal has two primary differences. First, it gives a time frame to both steps. Second, it lists the necessary tasks within the goal. You can use the 'steppingstone' goal system or the 'SMART' goal system or any other option that fits your personality; just make sure that you give everything a time frame or due date and understand all the tasks involved with completing that goal.

What Happens When You Don't Have a Plan?

Disaster; absolute and utter disaster. While there are many things in your life that you can simply "wing" or go with the flow, homesteading is not one of them. You must plan for the season you're in, and the season ahead of you. You must plan how you'll store your harvest for months to come, and what you might do to improve efficiency in day-to-day chores. If you can't see the forest for the trees, you'll be lost.

Imagine if you went out and bought chickens today but didn't have a coop. Chickens have a lot of natural predators, and chicks are tiny. A hawk could easily come and clear out your new flock, or a coyote could get them overnight. Or, imagine if you bought a trough garden today and threw some general seeds in it, but then realized that you have a two-week vacation coming up, and didn't make plans for anyone to care for the seedlings.

Fortunately, you can plan around everything. Plan around your vacations, your weekend plans, your time spent at work, or how the weather changes with the seasons. Unfortunately, however, there will be times when you're planning doesn't quite work out. Things change, the unexpected happens. But still, it is always better to have a plan and adapt later, rather than to not have a plan at all.

"By failing to prepare, you're preparing to fail." - Benjamin Franklin

Quick Considerations for Your Layout Plan

In chapter two, we covered a lot of elements that you should carefully consider before you even start planning. We won't go through them all again, but instead, we will leave you with a shortlist

that you can refer back to quickly throughout the remainder of this chapter:
- Water access
- Sunshine exposure and shade coverage
- Land grade (will you need to level land?)
- Trees and existing structures that cannot be moved

Mapping Your Mini-Farm Layout

Everyone has a restriction when it comes to their land; even if you have acres and acres of property, there are restrictions. However, a limitation of land or space doesn't mean that you can't homestead. In fact, many people successfully homestead on less than an acre, or even only a quarter of an acre of land. Even if you only have a small square of a backyard, you have a lot of opportunities to build up your homestead.

To start planning how you will use your land, follow these steps:

1. Measure the space in your yard and start creating a map.

2. Mark out how far away you have access to electricity through outlets, noting where you can occasionally use extension cords.

3. Mark out on your "map" any large, already existing, structures (play centers, gazebos, sheds, etc.).

4. Mark on your map where you already have water access

5. If you have a patio, mark where the cement ends, and the yard begins

Then consider how much space you'll give to each aspect of your homestead. Think about how you answered the questions above and take a look at your map. Then use a few average sizes of structures to help you plan out your space.

Typical Average Sizes to Keep in Mind
- Most trough gardens are 4' x 8' or 4' x 12' – Trough gardens can also have multiple tiers or levels, a bonus space-saving tip! (May need a lot of sun.)
- Chicken coops – Most chicken coops (comfortable for up to 10 chickens) are 4' x 4' or 4' x 8' with a chicken run of about 4' x 8'. (Requires sun and shade.)

- Goat pens and pasture – Goats need a lot of space. You can opt for a night-time "pen" of about 4' x 8' with a top, or a full pen of 10' x 6'. (Requires sun and shade.)
  - Milking cow pasture – 15 square feet per cow, or
  - Fruit trees – each tree needs about 20' x 20'
  - Berry bushes – plant about 2' to 2.5' apart
- Other elements such as alfalfa crops, corn, and compost piles you can size to your needs.

When making your map, know that you don't need a lot of backyard space unless you have children. Even then, children love playing around animals, trees, and a garden. You may set aside some space for a lawn, sitting area, or play area, but you can, without a doubt, create a self-sustaining homestead on a quarter of an acre. The benefit of having trough gardens and flexible fencing designs is that you can move some things around as needed. Now your crops, chicken coop, trees, and bushes aren't so easily moved. Just be sure that when you go through your initial planning, you're putting everything in an area that meets all of its needs so that you're not constantly moving things around. It is always easier to over-plan and do things right than to have to try to move a chicken coop three months later when you realize it has no natural shade in the daytime. However, some of your household needs and limitations may affect your land use as well. For example, if you need chickens, then without a doubt, you're dedicating a fair amount of space to a chicken coop and run. Additionally, if you don't have the means to preserve all of your products, then you may want to scale down your first-year goals to ensure you're not overrun with unused produce, dairy, and eggs.

Sample Backyard Homestead Layouts

As you go through the layouts, keep in mind that you can level land, remove trees, and add trees or awnings for shade. If you find yourself thinking, "That won't work," you can try again.

1/4-Acre Homesteads

On a quarter of an acre, you can manage a small herb garden as close to your backdoor as possible, and if you have space next to that, you can plant two or three berry bushes. They're generally not large and can do with partial sun and partial shade. Then, within your yard, you should be able to manage three planter boxes, or three stretches of 4'x4', 4'x6', or 4'x8' gardens. With your property, you should still have room for either two fruit trees, a goat pasture, or a single cow pasture. Finally, you should have room for a 4'x4' chicken coop with an additional 4' for a chicken run.

That kind of setup should not consume so much of your yard that you can't have room for your kids to play outside or a nice sitting area. The idea, however, is to keep your plants as close to the backdoor as possible so that you can place your animals further out. The chicken area may be the only thing you want to change as it can be nice to have the coop near an outdoor outlet near the side of the house. Most houses have one or two weather-safe outlets facing into the backyard either on the back wall or on the sidewall. Those can be helpful for lamps and water heaters.

An alternative setup is to divide your grassy area into two pastures, one containing the chicken coop. Both pastures can contain fruit trees. Then, on the cement area of your back yard, you can have smaller planter boxes to fit within your patio area.

1/3-Acre Homesteads

With a one-third acre, you have a lot more space, but still, need to be efficient with your planning. One option is to segment off an area four feet deep along the entire backstretch of your property line and use that for a pasture either for a goat, cow, or pig. On the other side of the pasture, you could put your chicken coop with rabbit cages on the other side of the chickens. Remember that rabbits are more skittish than chickens, so it's best to give them some space from larger animals no matter how good-natured they are.

In the largest and sunniest area of your yard, place your garden. You can opt to dig into the ground or use planter boxes. Just ensure that you have enough space to walk, weed, and harvest. Again, keep your herb garden as close to the house as possible. Consider placing trees or berry bushes on the least utilized section of the yard. This style of setup should leave you with enough space for a swing-set or play area and maybe even a fire pit. You can have your homestead and enjoy your backyard too!

1/2-Acre Homesteads

Now you have a lot of room! A half of an acre might not seem like much, but you're running a mini-farm, not a mass production farm, and you have more than enough space to enjoy every element of homesteading.

Start by planning your orchard. The good thing about orchards is that they don't need level ground. If possible, keep your chicken coop as close to your orchard as possible, it's great natural shade and keeps temperatures down during summer months. Along with the poultry area, you can keep rabbits as well. Do try to keep goats away from trees, if possible, as they like to eat the tree itself, not just the leaves.

Then, use a larger portion of your level and sunny area for vegetables, alfalfa, and berries. You can grow in rows or even fence them off from one another. Then you should have a rectangular area that you can segment off for a goat or cow pasture. Try to keep these further away from the house, and you should have room for a large compost bin near the pastures.

As always, herb gardens are best nearer the house, but when you have gardens this large, you might consider planting your herbs within your garden to keep out pests. Many herbs can deter bugs that could otherwise devastate your garden, and with a larger garden, you need all the help you can get.

1-Acre Homesteads

Oh, the things you can do with a whole acre of property! Start with your herb garden, or again, utilize your herbs for low-level pest control in your garden area. You may also aim to separate your seasonal garden from your perennial garden. Using planter boxes is still nice as it can reduce the amount of time you spent stooped over, but it is also nice to work right into the ground.

Then carve out a back corner of your property for compost. With this much land, you can get away with an open-air compost pile so long as it doesn't bother your neighbors. Then, you can have an orchard area. If your orchard is properly fenced, your orchard area can double as an open-air chicken run; place the chicken coop inside the orchard. Chickens love to run around and explore, and most breeds don't fly well, but if you notice one or two of them getting out, you can simply clip off the final corner feathers of their wings. If you're raising chicken for meat, this is exceptionally good.

With your orchard and garden areas set up, you can focus on your pastures. Again, within the confines of your animal zoning, you should be able to get away with sheep, goats, and a cow or two. Sheep and goats do well together but don't keep them with the cows because they can exchange unwanted gastrointestinal parasites that do serious damage to your cows.

Regardless of Size

Before moving on there is one last note when it comes to planning out your homestead: nearly everything is possible. Some successful homesteaders work with 1/8th of an acre of land. They use hanging gardens, have tiny chicken coops for two or three chickens, and use a compost bin. Don't buy into the idea that you need a massive amount of space to homestead. You may need to start small and then grow later.

Near the end of this book, we have a chapter on growing your homestead, and that may mean growing physically or adding new elements. But there are almost always ways to get started with what you have now. It's one of the great lessons of homesteading; there is always a way to "make do."

Making the Most of Your Land

There are many ways that you can get multi-functional use from your land, although again, it takes a bit of planning to execute effectively. Your pastures, coops, orchards, berries, and gardens don't all need separate spaces. Additionally, you can make the flow easier for harvesting and maintenance, ensuring that you use your land in the most efficient manner possible.

For example, one of the sample backyard homestead layouts explained above made the orchard part of the cow pasture. That was possible because the trees needed about 20 square feet each, and the cows needed a pasture of 10'x10' meaning that you could have two trees along with your two cows. Cows and orchards work well together because unlike goats, your cows shouldn't try to eat the bark or low hanging branches of your trees (although they do like to rub up against them.)

Another common pairing is to keep sheep and goats together. Their temperaments mix well, although you might consider castrating males to discourage crossbreeding, as it rarely works out well.

We can go over some examples of making your flow easier for working and harvesting. Initially, many people choose to keep their herb garden on a kitchen windowsill as it makes the herbs easily accessible and doesn't take up outdoor space. Another option is to arrange your orchard or berry bushes on the side of the yard that doesn't get much foot traffic, as you'll harvest from these plants less often. You might also keep your pastures or pens close to your compost pile. Finally, consider how you feed and rotate through your harvest. Do you give the bunnies fresh vegetables? Why not sit them right near your garden?

Sitting down and mapping out your plan can quickly seem overwhelming, but it's important to understand that even with a 1/4-acre of land, there are a thousand and one ways to plan your homestead successfully. Don't get overwhelmed and remember that if necessary, you can change the layout. Although changing the layout is a hassle, it's possible.

Chapter 4: Selecting Your Seed Stock and Cultivars

Your seeds and cultivars will primarily dictate what you gain from your homestead. The decisions you make here will determine most of the plant-based portion of your diet. You can choose from a greater variety of seed and plant options than you might find in the store. However, many factors go into making these decisions. The first step is to decide if you'll use seeds, cultivars, or a blend of both.

What is the Difference between Seeds and Cultivars?

Seeds are pretty straightforward. They are seeds. Some are extremely expensive, and it's generally best that you get them from a reputable seed supplier rather than the paper packets you can find in stores. If paper packets have worked for you in the past, then stick with what works. Otherwise, you might jump online to explore the options in seeds after you decide what exactly you want to grow.

Cultivars, however, are an entirely different approach to planting. Cultivars come from the plant itself; they're a portion of a tree, a trimming from a plant, or something similar. You can do it with all kinds of fruit and vegetables; for example, you can grow a new celery plant from the heart of an old one. However, cultivars with the exclusion of fruit trees, are often a disappointment. Typically, these plants can't sustain their life or produce high-value vegetables. Additionally, if you use the seeds from these plants, they often produce the same lackluster result. Now cultivars can happen naturally. However, many of the cultivars that you'll come across on the market today are plants that are patented and licensed, meaning that you're not purchasing a natural product of a plant, but something created for this very purpose. Now some of these purposes make sense. One example is the Burning Bush shrub, which through cultivation, making it a cultivar, has become more compact.

Perhaps the best analogy to explain the difference between seeds and cultivars is dog breeding. Seeds are your very natural one-dog-meets-another-and-they-have-puppies scenario. Cultivars, or modern cultivars, are more like puppy mills. Through excessive inbreeding and controlled genes, you produce an organism with very specific traits. Unfortunately, the traits have become so specific that they are unstable.

As a new homesteader, you may choose to use a blend of seeds and cultivars. It may be easier to get started with cultivars even if their lifespan may not be exceptionally fruitful or long. There may also be the challenge of deciding exactly which seeds you want right away; using cultivars for one season at a time can help delay that decision.

Building a Garden for Your Season and Climate

It would be wonderful if the sky were the limit when it came to gardening, but everyone has to take into consideration the season and the climate. As a new homesteader, it is reasonable to dread the upcoming vicious winter months that tend to wipe out gardens. However, there are a wide variety of very hardy winter vegetables and crop options.

We've tried to break your options down within these restrictions as much as possible, so it's easy to refer back to this chapter when you're planning your seasonal crops. Now, although there many different climates, because of new technology and improved agriculture methods, it is possible to grow things that wouldn't normally do well in your environment. While you may not be able to grow an avocado tree in the New Mexico desert with ease, it could be possible.

Spring
- Asparagus
- Avocados
- Broccoli
- Cabbage
- Carrots
- Celery
- Collard greens
- Radishes
- Rhubarb
- Strawberries
- Swiss Chard
- Onions
- Mushrooms
- Lettuce
- Garlic
- Peas

Summer
- Okra
- Lima beans
- Raspberries
- Strawberries
- Summer squash
- Tomatillo
- Tomatoes
- Zucchini
- Eggplant
- Corn
- Garlic
- Cherries
- Celery

- Carrots
- Cantaloupe
- Blueberries
- Blackberries
- Bell peppers

Fall: (Nearly All Summer Crops are Suitable for Fall as Well)
- Potatoes
- Pears
- Pumpkins
- Rutabagas
- Sweet potatoes
- Yams
- Swiss chard
- Cranberries
- Ginger

Winter
- Carrots
- Celery
- Collard greens
- Kale
- Leeks
- Onions
- Pumpkins
- Swiss chard
- Winter squash
- Turnips

10 Perennial Vegetables to Grow Year-Round

Some plants are perennial, which means that they can produce year-round, and often they can produce for more than two years. These are often the vegetables and grains that you find in most modern diets.

So, what can you grow almost anywhere and year-round? These ten vegetables will grow at any time of year when properly cared for:

- Tomatoes – They can grow for years but can't survive a harsh winter (with full ground freeze). You can bring your tomatoes indoors during the winter or use weather-safe external heating elements.
- Peppers – They survive almost every climate but may need to come inside during the winter.
- Eggplants – Vegetables that will grow year-round. However, they are often treated as an annual plant.
- Okra – Can grow as high as 7-feet tall
- Chayote squash – A vine vegetable that goes dormant through the winter but produces from the beginning of spring to the end of fall.
- Horseradish – A rooted plant that usually gets harvested in winter for curing bad colds, something you can use year-round.
- Onions – Some varieties will grow year-round, including the perennial leeks, Egyptian walking onions, and perlite onions.
- Artichokes – Specifically the Jerusalem artichoke, it's a very hardy plant similar to potatoes. But be careful, they can grow and spread like wildfire; they may need their own container so as not to choke out your other plants.
- Radicchio – An all-star in salads and similar to cabbage, this plant wants sun and will reappear every spring, although it goes dormant in fall and winter.
- Kale – Grows well in hot and cold weather and is generally referred to as a super crop. Not to mention that it's packed with nutrients.

Keep in mind that you may not want to grow these year-round vegetables, or you may need to segment your perennial garden from your seasonal garden.

Plants That Only Grow in Certain Climates

It might be surprising to learn that tomatoes weren't originally native to Italy. In fact, they made their way to Italy by way of a Spanish vessel that had come from Peru. Until tomatoes made their way to Europe, they only thrived in the Peruvian climate. Now they've been bred to be so hardy that they are one of the go-to plants for new gardeners.

There are some plants, however, that are just too difficult to grow; mostly humid or tropical plants. Things like Asian greens, Chinese cabbages, Bok Choi, and tropical lettuce such as salad mallow, and even taro only do well in hot weather and high humidity.

What Can Flowers Do for Your Garden?

Flower gardens are beautiful, and vegetable gardens are useful, but why keep them apart? Few beginner growers realize the full potential of having flowers within your garden. They have exceptional benefits and can help you better develop your green thumb as they do require a bit more attention than most beginning vegetables.

Flowers serve three primary purposes in a garden:

- Promote pollination – resulting in higher yields and longer plant life
- Act as a decoy to deter pests – aphids and other pests often prefer flowers over vegetables.
- Attract predatory insects – bring in the insects that prey on aphids and other garden pests.

Flowers attract more pollinating insects which can not only help fertilize the flowers, but also tomatoes, beans, zucchini, peas, and any crops that rely on pollination. And they act as a bit of a sacrifice. If given the option between your tomatoes and cosmos, those aphids will flock to the flowers. Then you have predatory insects such as wasps and hoverflies that will eat aphids and nearly any other insect they can prey upon.

Know Your Seed Varieties

Typically, when discussing seed varieties, people are talking about the different plant life they have on their property. However, there are different types of actual seeds that you may purchase for planting. This is the information that you'll see on seed labels, and it can be a bit difficult to understand at first. But knowing what you're buying is pretty important.

Open-Pollinated
These seeds are from plants that naturally bred in a field or general growth environment. Usually, these strains are much more stable because they've been bred generation after generation, and they should produce plants similar to their parent.

Heirloom
These are open-pollinated plants that were bred for specific traits for a minimum of 50 years. It is why heirloom tomato varieties are often so easy to distinguish. Heirlooms are well-known for their hardiness, which can make them a better choice for people who haven't gardened previously.

Hybrid
Hybrids use purposeful breeding to crossbreed two different plants or even two different species. However, hybrids are altered in the field through a "natural" means of pollination and cultivation. Hybrids do carry the risk of being sterile, and they may not breed "true," meaning that they may not produce exactly what the breeder or grower intended.

GMO
GMO is exactly what you probably suspect it is; these are Genetically Modified Organisms. They are made in a laboratory and are typically patented, resulting in brand name labels, and it is a challenge to find these on the home growing market.

Cell-Fusion CMS Treated
A method of genetically altering the seed through a type of GMO process. The modified trait is eliminated from future genetic possibilities, which means that it comes from a GMO, but it does not share the same genetic modifications as the parent plant.

Why is knowing all of this about plants and seeds important? As noted earlier, heirlooms can be easier to grow. Additionally, hybrids may carry a higher-nutrient density or a better disposition for your climate. Although these are details that you may not want to concern yourself with during your first season, it is something to consider as you look into seed buying more deeply.

Use Your Personal Preferences to Plan Your Seed Stock

Tomatoes are generally easy to grow in a wide variety of climates and can grow year-round if handled correctly. But, if you don't like tomatoes, don't grow them. Think about what you eat now and what you would like to introduce into your diet. Do try to be as diverse as possible and give some thought to planting different varieties within the same family, such as gold potatoes and red potatoes.

But in the end, you don't want to have a garden full of things you don't like to eat. Part of your garden's role in your homestead is to cultivate self-sustainability within your household, meaning fewer trips to the grocery store or dining out. Keep in mind that your garden may not just include the vegetables that take center stage on your dinner plate. Many grow kales purely for juicing or smoothies, and others grow peppers to season and spice up their cooking. Even the flowers mentioned earlier are largely edible. For example, clover and marigold are both edible but have very different roles on a table.

Use your personal taste to lay out the foundation of what you would like to see in your garden. Then determine what seasons those choices thrive in, and if there are additional plants you can add to your garden to support their growth and expand the variety of options you have available in your kitchen.

It might seem like all this research into seeds is unnecessary, or maybe overkill. However, you'll save yourself a ton of time and effort if you put your energy into choosing plants that you enjoy eating, that can be harvested in an easy-to-manage rotation, and that will hold up better to disease.

Chapter 5: How to Select Chickens and Build a Coop

Chickens can be an extremely valuable element of any homestead. They not only produce eggs, but they also provide fertilizer and make excellent pets. However, like any other animal, they entail quite a bit of work. It's not as easy as sticking them into the coop and checking for eggs every few days. They require daily care, can become sick, and may need special help in either cold or hot seasons. The presence of eggs can also attract unwanted creatures onto your homesteads such as snakes, skunks, opossums, rats, raccoons, and crows.

Although there is the risk of pests, chickens are well worth the investment and position within your homestead. What you'll need to do is plan how you will house them, feed them, and keep their environments clean. How you'll go about planning these things typically won't change based on what type of chickens you have.

Selecting the Right Chickens for Your Homestead

When choosing your chickens, you'll want to consider the volume of egg production, how resilient they are, and their abilities to promote your homestead in other ways. For example, some chickens are excellent for pest control. Although they may invite in unwanted small mammals, they can control bugs on the property. Other chickens are better for meat production while still offering egg production.

The three primary types of chickens we'll explore here are the heritage breeds, the alternative breeds, and "momma hen" breeds.

Heritage Breeds

Typically, your heritage breeds are the more common chicken breeds. Heritage breeds include the White Leghorn, the Rhode Island Red, and the Black Australorp. They do have some basic differences, especially when it comes to production and temperament. They're easy to distinguish by color and size.

Usually, homesteaders will have at least one heritage variety, and many beginners will have all three. The purpose of starting only with heritage breeds is that they're all pretty hardy. However, everyone has their preferences, and bringing in all three breeds is like a bit of an experiment to see what options fit you best.

White Leghorns

White Leghorns, as in the famous cartoon chicken Foghorn Leghorn, are possibly the most common type of chicken. They are your stereotypical white-feathered chicken with a yellow beak and red comb or craw. They lay between 250 and 300 eggs per year, and their egg-laying largely depends on climate and security. They are perhaps the most consistent chicken breed when it comes to egg production.

White Leghorns typically have a docile demeanor. Their temperament is calm, but largely they like to be left alone; they're not the type of chicken you buy for animal support or to serve as a pet. White Leghorn roosters can become aggressive.

Rhode Island Reds

These chickens lay the coveted brown eggs and regularly produce about 280 eggs per year. They're a great choice for first-time homesteaders because they are a very resilient breed. They stand up to both cold and warm weather well. You can easily recognize them for their pretty red feathers, and they're generally smaller and stouter than Leghorns.

These chickens are extremely well tempered, although again, the roosters can become aggressive. Rhode Island Reds are also great foragers and actively go after insects. If you're looking for something with a better temper than a Leghorn and are willing to sacrifice some egg production, you might choose Rhode Island Reds.

Black Australorps

Australorps will lay between 200 and 240 eggs in a year, a slightly lower egg count than the other two heritage breeds. You can easily distinguish them by their black feathers with almost green highlights. They're generally pretty and can get rather large. They are rather gentle but can be timid as they tend to scare more easily than most other breeds.

Initially, the Black Australorps came from an English breed called Black Orpingtons to increase egg production without increasing the size of the bird or decreasing the quality of the meat. If you're looking for a bird for meat and egg production, then you should definitely consider the Black Australorp.

Alternative Breeds

These aren't heritage breeds, and often they're mixes of one or more breeds bred together for a specific purpose. Often the purpose is meat quality or hardiness when it comes to holding up against some weather conditions. These breeds are generally hardier, calmer, and more economical in that their production isn't shifted by their space. Alternative breeds are also great for urban settings. If you don't have a lot of land, these are a top choice.

California Whites

These chickens are egg production machines! They typically put out about 300 eggs per year and have very little fluctuation in production from season to season. They are winter hardy and do well with confinement. The confinement element is one thing that makes them so desirable in small environments. They lay white eggs. And they are smaller than your Leghorn varieties, although they're a mixed breed between a Leghorn and various other breeds.

Finally, the Whites are very quiet and docile. If you're worried about the noise level of your chickens, you might need some California Whites. If you know that your neighbors would have problems with louder flocks, a California White flock would be best. What deters most people who are new to chicken raising from California White's is that the hens are "broody," which means they want to sit on their eggs. You may see some aggression when you go to collect eggs, or have hens outright refusing to leave the nesting boxes.

Cinnamon Queens

Red, stout, and a high-production brown egg-layer. Because of its hybrid breeding, the Cinnamon Queen develops and begins laying quickly. They have feathers that go from dark red across the top of their body to light red underneath. Their legs are primarily yellow, and their beak is well-colored. They lay between 250 and 300 eggs per year, but they do stop producing earlier in life, which means that after a few years you may have a lot of retired hens that aren't producing but still draining homestead resources such as feed, water, and space.

Additionally, there is quite a bit of concern about Cinnamon Queen's health troubles. Many report that they die very early on, and it can be extremely unpleasant. These statements aren't a shock as Cinnamon Queens are a "designer" red-gene chicken, which is the equivalent to a designer dog breed that has been overbred into health problems.

Red and Black Sex Links

Red and Black Sex Link chickens are not inherently an alternative breed but a collection of smaller breeds. These breeds, including Cinnamon Queen and many others, were bred with the specific purpose of getting a high egg production. That means that they often lay well above 300 eggs per year. But, don't be fooled, higher egg production often comes with various health issues, bad temperaments, and high activity. They also don't do well at all in cold weather.

If you have a lot of land, then the high activity isn't a problem, but it is discouraging, particularly for new chicken farmers, when you don't know how to help the potential health problems. Of course, many of these chickens live full, disease-free lives. It's just one of the many possibilities to go over before you make your decision on which chickens to purchase.

Raising Chickens for Slaughter

Most of the chickens you would choose for egg-laying aren't the best options for meat production. The best options for meat production are the Cornish hens and the Rock chickens. Additionally, you might choose Freedom Rangers, which generally grow slower, or the Plymouth Barred Rock, which generally produces more meat than the Cornish or Rock varieties. However, the meat is not of the same quality.

There is a significant difference between chickens meant for meat production and chickens meant for egg production. When it comes to chickens meant for meat production, your heritage breeds are the Cornish hens, rock hens, and Freedom Rangers. These chickens are well known for their friendly demeanor and natural tendency to explore. They want to roam around; they don't want to be stuck in a small coop for the entirety of their lives.

When considering the choice of raising chickens for meat, you'll need to go through the following steps:

- Can you give these chickens a good life and a humane death?
- Can you financially provide for chickens that may not give back to the homestead for months?
- Will you raise heritage breeds or Cornish cross hybrids?

The first issue mentioned here can help you determine what type of chickens you choose if you're raising them for slaughter. If you cannot give chickens a good life and a humane death, then you should generally avoid raising chickens for meat. However, if you're worried about giving them a good life for the duration of a few years, that may change your perspective. Most chickens for meat production are humanely slaughtered before they reach eight months in age. You don't have to give this chick a home for two or three years. You simply have to give them food, water, and shelter for a few months. Then you'll need to worry about how you can humanely slaughter them. There are a few different tools to help farmers with this, and as you develop your homestead, you'll quickly learn that animal death is one of the elements you'll have to face on occasion.

When it comes to the financial elements, there are a few misconceptions. When you first start raising chickens, you'll come across one of the few times in homesteading where it is more expensive to have the homestead than to go to the grocery store. Your initial investment to raise chickens will involve a coop, access to water, feeders, and nesting boxes. Then you'll have your recurring expenses for the chickens, including water and chicken feed. If you calculate the cost through your first few months raising chickens for meat production, it will definitely seem as though spending $2.99 per pound for chicken thigh meat at the grocery store is cheaper. However, as you get into the ebb and flow of raising chickens for meat production, the initial costs and the recurring costs will level out.

So, will you raise heritage chickens or Cornish cross hybrids for meat production? Many people are encouraged to use heritage chickens for several reasons. First, their natural curiosity to explore and run around can help with pest control and dirt. Second, because they are running around, their meat often has a more natural taste. Finally, they often make great companion pets for other chickens and goats.

Cornish cross hybrids, however, are a different story. These chickens have been bred to sit, stand, and eat. They are not interested in interacting with other animals, or in exploring the yard. In fact, Cornish cross hybrids do best when they're kept in a very small confined space with around-the-clock low light. If you haven't guessed yet, those are exactly the conditions that chickens are raised under in questionably ethical mass production farms. They will often fall subject to disease, a heart attack caused by stress, and broken bones. The intentional breeding to produce Cornish cross hybrids has resulted in an unstable body structure.

Do You Need a Rooster for Hens to Lay Eggs?

A common misconception is that you need a rooster on the property for hens to lay eggs. Local feed store owners often perpetuate this belief, and there's a substantial amount of misinformation about this subject online as well.

A hen does not need a rooster to lay eggs. However, if you're planning to raise chickens, a rooster is absolutely necessary. The only thing that a rooster does is fertilize the eggs. However, many homesteaders believe that having a rooster on the property serves as a type of security for the hens or that perhaps the hens are more productive when a rooster is around because they feel that the environment is safer.

When deciding if you're going to have a rooster or not ask yourself these questions:

- Will I be raising baby chicks?
- Will my hens be near potential threats? (Even perceived threats such as a dog.)
- Do I want fertilized eggs?

Silkies and Brahmas – Momma Hens

We just briefly touched on the purpose of roosters on a homestead. Now let's touch on the role of momma hens. Whether you choose to use heritage or alternative chicken breeds for your egg production, it's not likely that those hens will sit on their eggs. If you do happen to have a particular chicken that is brooding, it's not necessarily a good thing. A brooding chicken may become aggressive if you attempt to collect eggs and may become depressed or stressed if you continue to remove their eggs. You don't want a brooding heritage or alternative breed hen. So, what do you do if you want to raise your own chickens?

The answer is to bring in one or two momma hens. Momma hens are usually Silkies or Brahmas. These are chickens that you probably won't rely on for egg production or meat production. What they do is mothering work. They sit on eggs, protect them, and they are very good-natured. They're so desirable that some people choose to keep them as pets.

Silkies

A silkie is well-known for its silk-like features and docile temperament, and they love being held. Silkies don't look like your normal chicken. They are very fluffy and usually grow too big, although certain sub-breeds may be larger than standard.

Brahmas

Brahma chickens, in contrast to Silkies, are typically much larger than your average chicken. In fact, one of their giant breeds had quite a bit of news attention as the chicken went in full height to about three feet tall. On average, a Brahma chicken will grow to about thirty inches tall and weigh over twelve pounds. They also have very long lifespans, with it taking nearly three years to reach their full size.

✳ Other Factors to Consider When Raising Chickens

Along with the types of chicken you have to choose between, you'll need to consider a few other factors. For example, if you have coyotes or wolves, you'll want to ensure that you have a very secure chicken coop. Additionally, you'll need to plan for your egg storage. It's not likely that you'll eat hundreds or even thousands of eggs in a year. Some people give them away, others sell them in local farmer's markets, while some store them by pickling or freezing.

These are just a few factors to consider, and they might help you determine what type of coop to build. For example, if you get a lot of rain, then you should seriously consider a chicken coop that is raised a few feet off the ground, so it's not flooded frequently.

Build a Chicken Coop

Every chicken coop has the same basic elements. You will create a structure to protect your chickens from bad weather and give them a safe space to lay their eggs. Your chicken coop does not need to be complex or elaborate. In fact, the simpler the chicken coop is, the easier it is to maintain. It is nice to imagine giving your chickens a lush mansion with every add-on imaginable, but that's not reasonable.

You'll want to get started by determining how many chickens you'll have. You want to give each chicken about four square feet of space to walk around. There is also the debate on the number of nesting boxes you need. Chickens will share nesting spaces, but if you plan on growing your flock later, it might be better to design in more nesting spaces earlier on than to try to add them in the future.

There aren't set names for the different styles of chicken coops, but we can lay out a few basic shapes for you to get a feeling of what options are available. The most common style of a chicken coop is a shed frame; the coop itself simply looks like an outdoor shed, with an outdoor wire space set next to it. There is also the a-frame style, which looks a bit more like a propped-up tent. You can create a chicken coop in a gazebo style which is typically all open across the sides, and then there is the off the ground "Palace" structure. The most functional and the most economical for space is the shed style structure, so that's what we'll cover here to help you learn how to build a chicken coop. If you are interested in an A-frame or gazebo style chicken coop, then you might browse around online for a pre-made structure or a set of plans. Building any structure other than your standard shed style might call for more advanced building skills. Of course, any skilled builder can create custom designed and uniquely shaped chicken coops that fit their yard.

After you decide how many chickens you will keep and the style of shed that you would like, you'll need to decide where to place it in your yard. When you're working with backyard homesteading or creating a mini-farm, location is a really big deal. Your flock has certain demands, and that might change how you arrange your backyard homestead. Your flock will need sunshine, access to shade, good airflow, and low noise levels, and you'll need easy access so you can get in and out comfortably. Try to consider a few different locations and spend some time in those areas first to get a feel for the noise level and airflow.

Next, you'll want to plan out your coop, and when you're using a basic shared structure, it is as simple as four walls, a floor, a roof, a caged outside region, nesting boxes, and a door. However, you will need windows or slats for ventilation, and a designated spot for your feeder and waterer.

The extras that you might consider adding into your chicken coop involve a perch area, dust bath, lighting, and poop boards. If you're considering adding in any extras, prioritize the lighting and the poop boards. Lighting is an element that can help improve egg production, particularly during the winter months, and what you want is to bring UVA and UVB lighting directly into the enclosed area of the coop. Having lights in the coop means you need access to electricity, and if you have harsh winters, not only for lighting but for water heaters. If at all possible, ensure that you can get electricity to your chicken coop. Now poop boards are a small extra that doesn't take much work and can save you a lot of time in maintaining your homestead. A poop board is placed below the perching area and should easily slide in and out of the chicken coop.

Once you have your plan sketched out, you'll be ready to select your materials. Most who are building their own coop prefer wood, and you don't have to worry about the type of wood so much with chicken coops. You can choose something affordable. However, there's no need to bring in wood such as Cedar that would stave off pests. The chickens will gladly welcome insect company. In addition to all wood materials, you will need chicken mesh or chicken wire. This type of wire is woven loosely enough that good airflow can get through it, but not so loosely that the chickens can escape.

The best possible size for most mini-farms is a 4'x4'x6' structure for ten chickens, and then an additional 4'x8' chicken coop run. There are countless free plan options that you can refer to when building. However, if you can set up a floor, four walls, a door, and a roof, you'll have no problem. Perhaps the best resource in this regard is the numerous DIY tutorial videos. Even with a written plan, if you're not familiar with building yet, this is a great place to get started, as it's best to watch someone build a structure or to get hands-on help.

If you're worried about getting your materials and equipment, note that you can rent most of what you need. Local hardware stores and even the larger chains will cut materials on-site and rent large tools. That means that you don't have to invest in a circular saw or heavy equipment. Chickens can play a substantial role in your homestead, and it's worth the effort to build them a good coop.

Chapter 6: Preparing Your Kitchen for a Homestead

Most people use their kitchen for general cooking and food storage. But a homestead goes far beyond general use. When you have a homestead, you must have some joy in your kitchen, because you're going to be using it for much more than general use. You won't occasionally be throwing something into the oven or turning on the crockpot the night before; instead, your kitchen will be used for other homesteading jobs besides cooking. You will use it for canning, jarring, other forms of food preservation, and even processing food from a raw state into another state, such as turning milk into yogurt.

Your kitchen will need to handle the storage of fruit, vegetables, and livestock goods with ease. That means you'll need to have all the necessary tools to process these goods, and then storage abilities to hold and manage them properly. We'll get further into long-term storage techniques in a later chapter; for now, we'll focus on what supplies you will need and how to get the most out of your kitchen's space.

When preparing your kitchen for a homestead, it should, of course, be highly functional, but it should also be a safe haven. To make sure that you can enjoy your kitchen and that you minimize any kitchen-oriented frustrations, start by making sure you have all the right supplies.

Checklist of Supplies

Part of homesteading is about learning to use what you have. You should have the basics, and then a few things that can generally help make life easier or your kitchen safer. This list has a few things that you could probably do without but that you probably won't want to go without when it comes time for cooking, organizing, and preparing food.

Before we dive right into the list, let's put a special note on quality. Buy what you can afford, but if possible, buy the best you can afford. It is far better to have a high-quality cast iron skillet and Dutch oven combination than a set of cheaper pans and a cheap Dutch oven. Also, when buying higher quality items, it typically means that you're going without optional items that could clutter your home. Then there is the element of care. When something is more expensive or higher quality, you generally care for it more. Again, cast iron is a prime example of this in action because cast-iron requires maintenance after every use, but that one pan or pot can last for over a hundred years! They last so long because the people using them know that maintaining them is vital.

So, what exactly do you need to get started? This list here lays out everything that would be nice to have in a kitchen. Typically, you'll want at least one of everything, and usually, you can make do with only one item for each purpose. For example, you don't necessarily need three sauté pans, even if they are of different sizes.

Kitchen Supplies List

- Knives - must-haves are a chef's knife, bread knife, and a cleaver. However, a full set with paring knives and steak knives is an excellent choice as well.
- Shears - kitchen shears and shears for breaking down poultry.

- Pots – A large pot for water-bath canning and making stock, but smaller pots are very useful as well.
- Wooden utensils – opt for a traditional spoon, slotted spoon, spatula, and pasta spoon. Wooden utensils are generally better for all types of cookware compared to their metal counterparts.
- Cast-iron – must have a skillet, but a Dutch oven can be extremely useful.
- Measuring cups – Any set will do; if you're baking a lot, a 1 ½ measuring cup is very useful.
- Strainers or china caps.
- Mixing bowls.
- Cutting boards.
- Kitchen scale.
- Rolling pin.
- Bread pans – most homesteaders make their own bread, and for that, bread pans are extremely useful.

Kitchen Equipment List
- Oven and range/stovetop.
- Refrigerator.
- Freezer – with homesteading, a chest freezer is exceptionally useful!
- Sink – Consider the amount of time you'll spend in your kitchen; a bigger sink can be a huge stress relief from feeling like the sink is always full.
- Mixer – Standing, mounted, or handheld options are all good options. If you want to bake a lot, consider investing in a Kitchen Aid or commercial model, it can save a substantial amount of time.
- Blender.
- Food processor – save time on all that chopping!
- Thermometer – for baking and candy making, get a candy thermometer, not just a meat thermometer.
- Scrap bucket or kitchen compost box.

Optional Kitchen Equipment – The Luxuries in a Homesteading Kitchen

- Bread maker/bread machine – most will prove and bake the bread.
- Pressure canner – do away with canning in a pot.
- Dehydrator.
- Meat grinder.
- Sausage maker.
- Pasta maker – add-on options for standing mixers.
- Meat slicer.
- Food saver (vacuum-packed sealing system) – can severely reduce freezer burn and demands for storage space.

How and if you use these tools is completely up to you. Do consider your personal preferences, but don't be afraid to step outside of your comfort zone. Many people that haven't used a mixer before may favor a hand mixer and eventually upgrade to a standing mixer. Just the same, it's likely that you've never used a pressure canner or a bread maker. Remember that part of the satisfaction of homesteading is trying new things and learning how to make your own goods rather than running to the grocery store. Self-sustainability will always call for additional learning and a bit of fun.

Homesteading Tools and Supplies for Your Kitchen

There are some tools that only homesteaders will need. They can be used for humane slaughter, storage solutions, and long-term preservation. These tools provide very specific functions that you will likely need even if you're doing the very basics of homesteading, such as gardening and keeping chickens.

Homesteading Kitchen Tools and Supplies

- Yogurt culture – comes in both dried and liquid forms.
- Electric yogurt maker – not a must-have, but certainly a nice addition to your kitchen.

- Yeast – for baking bread.
- Glass canning jars – getting a variety of sizes is important, you'll also need lids and rings.
- Sheet trays – the more, the better.
- Canisters – that will keep dry goods dry, and pests such as moths out, and reduce the likelihood of weevils.
- Supplies for cheese making – curd knife, cheese molds, cheese press, cheese draining mats, cheese wax, cheese wraps, and butter muslin.

These supplies aid in a lot of dairy handling and storage. Even if you don't have a dairy cow on your farm, you can use store-bought pasteurized milk for making yogurt, and cheese. If your goal is to one day have a dairy cow, you can certainly work on your yogurt and cheese making skills now to be prepared for when you have a substantial amount of milk in your home.

Specialty Kitchen Tools for a Homestead

Some homesteads require very specific tools for the kitchen or related to the kitchen. These tools are for more advanced homesteaders and may not directly apply to your initial homesteading plans.

For rabbit culling, a means to "remove from the herd," which can mean giving the rabbit a new home or using it for meat. Typically, when you hear homesteaders refer to culling or dispatching, it is the nicest possible way to replace the word slaughter. Many people do get attached to their animals and still use them for their intended purpose (meat production).

A specialty tool for dispatching or culling rabbits is called the Hopper Popper. This tool provides a humane way to dispatch the rabbit, and the smallest size available also works on chickens. Although this isn't particularly a "kitchen" tool, many people mount it either inside a shed or on the side of the house away from the remaining rabbits or chickens, and it is a solid alternative to less-pleasant ways to handle dispatching.

Composters are another specialty tool, and you can keep a separate kitchen compost and an outdoor compost. But, as a specialty tool, you might consider a closed-compost box which should help reduce any odors in your kitchen as it doesn't directly open to your compost within the box, but rather has a two-step drop process.

How to Get and Stay Organized

Getting organized is one thing; staying organized is another. But, with some good planning and storage solution options, you can make staying organized easy. As you go through what you'll need in terms of space, you'll be able to assess better how you can manipulate the kitchen space you have. There is absolutely no reason to do a complete kitchen renovation to start a homestead! However, you might consider adding shelves, a wire rack, and pantry storage solutions such as stacked shelving.

Step One: Assess Your Space

You'll want to carefully evaluate where and how you currently use your cabinets and any shelving in your kitchen. Pantries are prime spots for items that you use every day! Walk through your kitchen with a notepad and document what items you keep and where you keep them. That box of stuffing that will sit on your shelf for months until the next holiday rolls around certainly doesn't deserve prime pantry space. Your cupboards don't have to only hold plates and glasses.

After you have taken stock of your kitchen and your kitchen space, go through each item and determine how often you use it. If you really do reach for your chopped walnuts every morning because you love them with breakfast, then keep them out and available. But if you only use them once a week for baking, or even less frequently than that, consider moving them into an area that is less convenient to reach.

Step Two: Declutter

Clutter is nothing to be ashamed of. Everyone has it. But when you're preparing your kitchen to become a critical part of a homestead, it's time for a good cleaning out and doing away with all of your current clutter. Just keep in mind that no matter how hard you try, clutter will always resurface, so don't get discouraged if you need to declutter again in six-months.

When you're decluttering consider following these guides:
- Keep only one of the things you need (one 1-cup measuring cup, or one slotted spoon).
- Stack inside and stack up (stack your cups in your cupboard, stack your pots together too)
- Ask, "Do I have something else that does the same thing?"

o Forget the hot debate between having a punch bowl and a serving pitcher, or between having a rice cooker and a pot. Some things don't need a fancy device or a duplicate. Now is the time to eliminate the unnecessary (especially single-function) kitchen gadgets.
- Ask, "How often do I use this?"

o Make piles for reorganizing your kitchen based on how frequently you use items. Daily items deserve locations as close to the counters or as easily accessible as possible. Weekly items deserve the outlying space, and monthly items need to go somewhere hidden or tucked out of sight.
- Ask, "Where is the most logical spot for this item?"

o Make sure that your most-used utensils are where you need them the most, such as near your stove. Then consider keeping others like things together where they best serve their purpose.

The decluttering and reorganizing step isn't about throwing everything out. It is about making sure that what you have is either handy or logically stored.

Step Three: Organize Everything – Including Your Food Storage

Before you put away everything that you dug out during the decluttering step, mark your cabinets, cupboards, and pantry with what you would like to put there. It will help you avoid derailing and just putting things back where they always were. Don't be afraid to keep things on the counter if you really do use them every day. If you make rice every day with dinner, then leave your canister of rice easily accessible on the counter!

Tips for Organizing

• Store dry food in large clear containers or canisters so you can easily see how much you have.

• If you buy bulk, then keep a "kitchen container" in your kitchen and store the rest in a bulk storage area.

• Keep your like items together – cans go with cans, grains go with grains, beans go with beans, and so forth.

• Keep a printed inventory list on a clipboard hanging somewhere easy to see while you are in the kitchen. Then, when you've used all but the last of something, you can add it to your shopping list, make more, or re-plan your planting, so you don't drop in quantity so quickly.

• Don't be afraid to store things in different places; for example, if you use honey every day, but buy it in bulk, then keep your bulk supply tucked away and enough to last you through the week out where you can access it easily.

• Add wall shelves – you immediately add storage space, and with Mason jars or canisters, the storage solution can look pretty snazzy too.

• Add stacked storage in your pantry – with pantry stacking shelves or stacking drawers, you can nearly double your pantry space.

When working within your kitchen, you might need to reorganize a few times before you find a complete system that works for you. At this time, if you're not sure how often you'll use something or need to access it, use sticky notes. Put sticky notes on items and then remove them when you have used them. At the end of the week, anything without a sticky note deserves a prime spot. Then go through and do it again for the month with a different color of sticky notes on the already approved items, so you're not confusing your most used items with your frequently used items. You can do this to help you manage your storage rotation as well.

Ultimately, your kitchen will become the indoor hub of your homestead. Don't be afraid to make changes to your system if they're going to help you better track and monitor your inventory and easily access all of your kitchenware.

Chapter 7: Harvesting and Preserving the Fruits of Your Labor

Even with excellent planning skills, there's no way that you can eat your way through everything that comes out of your garden or coop daily. When you factor in that your chickens will probably lay one egg each per day, and then you'll probably have between four and six chickens, you'll end up eating four to six eggs a day. That's a quick recipe for high cholesterol and a boring diet. However, using modern and traditional methods of food preservation, you can ensure that your pantry and refrigerator are stocked with your favorites year-round.

Home food preservation techniques are tried and tested. Hundreds of generations have gone through with some of these techniques in the past and lived. Although they may seem new to you, or even completely foreign, give them a chance. You might learn that something that seemed scary is actually something you're good at. Canning, for example, scares a lot of people because of the risk of botulism and other illnesses arising from improper canning. But canning is also very easy, and you'll probably do it right on your first try. So, give these options a chance and take advantage of every opportunity to keep your food for as long as possible.

To get started, here is a list of different ways to store and preserve food:

- Canning – using a combination of pressure and natural interaction between the materials.
- Freezing.
- Dehydrating – simply running warm to hot air around fruit, vegetables, and meat to produce dried versions.
- Root cellar – originally an underground structure, although modern renditions have used sheds and above-ground structures, providing a cool and semi-moist condition similar to your refrigerator vegetable drawer.
- Pickling – preserving in vinegar or brine.
- Jams and jellies – When unopened, homemade jam can last between one and two years on a shelf.
- Salting meats – meat can last between 1 and 2 months when salted, even without refrigeration. Salting meats is an old-age method of food storage.
- Fermenting – the process of using yeast or grain to cultivate beneficial bacteria and prolong the life of food. Common examples of fermented food include sauerkraut and kimchi. Fermented foods stored in a cool dark location can last between 4 and 18 months.
- Water kefir – probiotic culture lasting about 2-3 weeks in the refrigerator and up to two months in the freezer.
- Milk kefir – fermented milk consistent with drinkable yogurt lasts about 2-3 weeks in the fridge or up to 2 months in the freezer.
- Jerky – dehydrated meat, usually good for 1-2 weeks
- Sausage and hamburger – easier to freeze and store in reasonably sized portions.

If any of these sticks out as a reasonable option, then it's time to put it into your homesteading plan. Below is an in-depth explanation of all of the most popular options for preserving and storing food for a homestead.

Canning

Canning food involves applying heat to the food while it's sealed within a jar, destroying microorganisms that would otherwise lead to food spoilage. You want to use a proper canning technique, and two well-used techniques to accomplish proper canning are water-bath canning and pressure canning. Other techniques are not reliable and may put the safety of the food at risk. With canning, in any case, it is important to not fully close the rings around the lids as it can result in the can appearing to be sealed when, in fact, it is not. Close your rings tightly, and then give them a gentle nudge to loosen them just a bit.

Water-Bath Canning

Learning about canning is where most homesteaders begin because all you need is a large pot, a lid, and a rack. For effective water-bath canning, you'll place your jars with the lids on in a pot of boiling water until the inside of the jars reach 212-degrees. The time that the jars must remain at that temperature varies based on what you're canning. This method works exceptionally well for fruit, pickles, tomatoes, and other very acidic foods.

Pressure Canning

With pressure canning, you need a pressure canner as a piece of equipment. The pressure canner creates a locked compartment filled with steam and pushes the internal temperature in the jars to 240 degrees. At the same time, it applies a specific pressure that is based on the weight within the device. On these devices, you'll see a gauge that indicates the weight. This method is best for vegetables, poultry, fish, and other meats.

Pickling

There is the traditional form of pickling, but because of recent developments, there is also quick pickling. You can pickle nearly any type of vegetable, and you can pickle boiled eggs. The process of pickling is generally straightforward. Place the cut vegetables in jars of vinegar or a vinegar mixture of water, vinegar, salt, possibly sugar, and a wide variety of spices. Most people use pickling spice no matter what, but you can also include garlic, peppers, dill, and more. Then, store them in the refrigerator.

If you're more worried about keeping your fridge space open, then you will need to pressure can them or give them a water-bath canning process to ensure that they're properly sealed.

Freezing Foods

Freezing food is about much more than throwing something into a "freezer-safe" bag. You'll want to use freezer paper; wrap meat in freezer paper and butcher's paper, and then seal it properly. And you'll want to ensure that you're reducing as much air exposure as possible. When you freeze anything, you want to reduce the air exposure, because it is very cold, dry air that "burns" your food and leads to quick decay while in the freezer. Also, be sure that you never over-stuff your freezer because it needs airflow to slow any damage to the fresh food.

Tips for Freezing

- Freeze food at the peak of freshness.
- Always wrap food tightly and in multiple layers before putting it into the freezer.
- Keep your freezer full, but not stuffed.
- Boil and blanch your vegetables before freezing.
- If possible, store in vacuum-sealed bags.

When freezing vegetables, it may feel counterintuitive to cook them first. But you only want to boil your vegetables for a maximum of three minutes and then immediately submerge them in an ice bath (blanching). This takes the vegetables to their ideal state, and then when they freeze, they should retain that state.

Freezing berries or fruit is a different situation; you can typically freeze fruit without any cooking or blanching. In fact, cooking immediately begins to break down fruits as they're much more sensitive than most vegetables, especially root vegetables. You may need to approach each fruit slightly differently, though, because you don't want just to throw them into a bag. Ideally, you will lay fruit out on sheets, allow them to freeze through completely, and then put them into the freezer with proper layers of protection to avoid freezer burn.

Meat can do very well in the freezer, but again, the important aspect is layers. Freezer paper can make a substantial difference in quality. Then there needs to be another layer, typically of plastic wrap or wax paper, and then finally, storing them in a freezer-safe enclosure such as a freezer-safe bag or container.

Root Cellars – What You Need to Know

There are different types of root cellars, and not all are made equal. The particular problem that people face today is zoning and permits. Because root cellars are traditionally underground and should be tall enough for you to at least crouch standing up, you may have a rough time avoiding lines, plumbing, and more in your yard. However, if you find a local contractor, they may be able to help you determine if you are okay with creating a root cellar on your property. Root cellars are well worth the investment as they can help keep food fresh and at its most natural state for an extended period for time.

Root cellars are what people used before refrigerators were widely used. Almost everything can be saved in a root cellar. You can store canned goods, jarred goods, medicine, and produce such as carrots, turnips, potatoes, pumpkins, squash, and more. The absolute best environment for a root cellar is between 32 and 40 degrees (F) with 85-95% humidity. Because the humidity levels are so high, there is a minimal loss of moisture from the food. The low temperatures keep the decomposition rate at a minimum. The result is that the foods stored in a root cellar release ethylene gas at a much slower rate than if they were in any other environment. That gas then escapes through the ventilation.

Now, you must keep fruit and vegetables separate because of the drastic variances in decay time. They each release ethylene at different rates, and storing them together can cause both the fruit and vegetables to deteriorate more quickly.

Extending the Life of Dairy

Often, dairy is short-lived, with most store-bought milk having a shelf-life of between five and seven days, whereas yogurt is usually stable for one or two weeks, and cheese can last in a freezer for between 6 and 8 months. If you have a milking cow on your homestead, it is well worth the effort to learn how to make cheese and yogurt to get the most out of your milk production.

It is important to mention here that pasteurizing milk does not make it last longer. Pasteurized milk will typically have a shelf life of a week or less, but organic milk treated in other methods can last longer. A method called UHT or Ultra-High Temperature pasteurization allows the milk to remain shelf-stable, when properly refrigerated, for up to six months. UHT calls for super-heating the milk to 280 degrees (F) for two to four seconds and then rapidly cooling it back to 39 degrees, which kills any bacteria.

Unfortunately, at this time, there is no fool-proof way to accomplish this at home. Some use pressure cookers, and others use "Instant Pot" pressure cookers, but the result is the same, the milk tastes cooked because it is so difficult to chill it at home rapidly. It is generally recommended to avoid trying to UHT at home. However, there is hope among the homesteading community that there will soon be more options available for those who want to UHT at home. Maybe a new gadget or device that will assist in both the heating and the cooling, but as of 2020, the technology just isn't available on a residential scale.

Home Food Preservation Safety

Always ensure that you're focusing on safety. Canned foods come with the risk of botulism and other illnesses, as well as inherent bacterial growth and fungus. Pickling, when not done correctly, can lead to sour vegetables and wasted shelf space. Every method of food preservation comes with risk, even when you simply put things in the refrigerator.

When opening any food product that was stored for a while, smell it and explore it visually for signs of quality deterioration or decay.

Ideally, these methods of preservation will lock your products in time at the peak of their freshness or turn them into another food product, such as a fresh peach to jarred peach slices. These preservation methods can help you keep some of your crops in stock all year. Peaches make a great example because they only ripen through the summer, but with freezing, jarring, and making jams, you can use up your delicious peach stock all year.

Explore the different preservation options and see what you can manage in your kitchen and with your dedicated storage areas. There are more options available, too, if you're looking to break past the beginning level of homesteading and into the more advanced methods of food storage and preservation.

Chapter 8: Making a Profit from Your Homestead

Most people don't start a homestead with the dream of making a profit from their land. In fact, most people start out just hoping to curb some of their grocery bills and live a more self-sustaining lifestyle. But you can make the dream of living off of your homestead a reality. All of these methods of making a profit from your homestead do require work and dedication. However, they can also be very feasible ways of making money from something you're already doing.

If you were still in the planning phase of creating your homestead, then you might create a type of business plan to assess different ways that making a profit might fit into your homestead designs. Even people who are working on only a half or quarter of an acre can find many ways to cultivate a profit and a beautiful garden. Keep in mind that every homestead will face unique limitations, and your community may play a part in what works and what does not work for you.

Branding Your Homestead

If you're going to have any products that could generate revenue, you need a brand. A brand provides people with a way of associating with your homestead and products. There are countless examples of outstanding brands out there in the world, but your brand must represent your lifestyle.

When creating a brand, consider what values drove you to eventually commit to growing your own homestead. Sharing your story about how you became a homesteader and how you developed into a business could be very important for your customers. Generally, customers, even those who are interested in organic or homegrown products, want to understand the business behind the product. Giving your future customers a bit of insight into your life and your values can have a dramatic impact on your business.

What you want to achieve is what marketers call organic branding, a brand that develops as a result of the meaning and purpose of the product. It means that the brand has a unique voice, an attitude, and a set of views on ethics and cultural elements within the community. As the person selling goods, you're the one who will determine all of these things.

Branding does not mean that you need to have customized stickers, business cards, packaging, or cheesy commercials. While it certainly is nice to be able to sell T-shirts or to slap on a sticker with your homestead logo or a fun name you've given to your homestead, it isn't necessary. You simply need a name, an image, and an attitude to attach to a stall at a local farmer's market or an online craft shop. No matter what the platform or what products you're selling, you'll need some branding.

Selling Your Goods

Selling goods is the most direct way to make money from your homestead. It's a great way to get rid of excess inventory, and it can help reduce the time that your harvest sits on your shelves. If you know that you're going to have a plentiful amount of harvest every season, then there's no reason not to sell what you don't need for your household. The great news is that you can sell almost anything that you grow at home. As long as what you're selling is legal in your area, then it may be as simple as finding a local farmers' market and completing an application with your city or County officials. However, there are areas and there are items that do have legal restrictions.

We'll get into more details about legal restrictions a little bit further into this chapter, but to give a quick example, raw milk is one of the things that are illegal to sell or distribute on a national level. U.S. Federal guidelines given by U.S. Food and Drug administration ban the sale of raw milk, and the solution to selling milk would be to pasteurize it. Many legal restrictions on selling food or goods from a homestead have a clear-cut solution, so don't get discouraged if you see that there might be a few obstacles in your way.

What to Sell

So, what can you sell? You can sell almost anything, but here is a long list of things that are available on almost every homestead.

- Sell extra produce
- Sell seedlings
- Sell compost and compost materials
- Sell manure (bunny droppings, cow droppings)
- Sell your flowers
- Sell farm-fresh eggs
- Sell baby chicks
- Bottle and sell goat milk
- Bottle and sell cow milk
- Sell homemade butter
- Sell jerky
- Sell fresh herbs
- Sell dried herbs in premade spice mixtures
- Sell large poultry such as geese or ducks for hunting
- Sell potted plants
- Make and sell specialty pasta or pesto

Selling what you produce on your homestead is one thing, but you can also use it as another selling platform. If you have space for a pumpkin patch, it is very reasonable to open up a side gate to your pumpkin patch and charge neighbors to pick their own. Or you can do the same thing year-round with a U-pick farm where people throughout your community can enter through a side gate and then pick vegetables at their leisure.

There are some products that you can sell that would be considered special to that particular homestead. Here are some examples of homestead specialties that don't fit the mold for every homestead but can certainly be accessible products from your homestead.

- Honey from your bees
- Beeswax products
- Raise animals for slaughter for other people (similar to leasing out a pasture)
- Fishing on-site (if you have a fish farm)
- Fish (if you have a fish farm)
- Fishing bait (cultivated insect-life)
- Raising working dogs (more on this in Chapter 12)
- Building vertical gardens

All of these items refer to add-ons to a basic homestead. Not every homesteader raises bees, but those who do can benefit greatly from their honey and beeswax products. Additionally, not everyone is involved in aquaponics, but if you have a fishpond, then you have access to a wider variety of products to use to make money off of your homestead.

Raising animals, in particular, is another great way to make money from a homestead without technically selling a product. What you're selling at this point is a lease on pasture or herd-sharing, and the time spent raising and caring for the animals. Many people would love to have a home-raised cow or pig for fresh organic beef and pork at home, but don't have space or can't manage the maintenance for the animal. As a homesteader, you're equipped to do just that. There's also the option of raising working animals. For example, working dogs don't produce meat, but they are exceptionally helpful on farms and homesteads, and not every homesteader has the patience to raise their own working dogs.

Crafting and Creating

It's probably a safe bet to say that if you can build and sustain a homestead, you might be pretty crafty too. Crafting goods is one of the really fun elements of homesteading where you take raw goods or your excess materials and make something completely yours. Crafting is also built into the self-sustaining element of a homestead, where you may need to, for example, build a chicken coop instead of purchase one. When you turn to craft and creating, you're doing a lot more than selling raw or nearly raw goods.

Sell these to make an extra bit of income from your homestead:
- Sell jams, jellies, or preserves.
- Sell candles.
- Sell Chapstick or other beeswax items.
- Make your own luscious hair and skin products from all-natural ingredients.
- Sell homemade soaps.
- Make fishing lures out of chicken feathers.
- Repurpose wood into different pieces of furniture or home décor.
- Sell crochet or knitting projects.
- Sell quilts and other simple-living luxuries.

This list is not all-inclusive, and you can add nearly anything that you can think of to it if you can make it on your homestead or in your kitchen. The idea, of course, is to use goods that you've created on your homestead to generate profit with a bit of creative flair. For example, homemade hair and skin products have a big market on websites such as Etsy because people want alternatives to the chemical-filled products you find on the shelves in stores. Of course, nearly everything on this list entails a skill you may need to learn. Skills like candle or soap making have been all but lost in the last couple of centuries. However, once you learn how to make them, you can do it again and again and continue to generate profit from that same skill set.

Craft and Specialty Fairs

All of the platforms listed in the section below are still options for when it comes to selling homemade goods. Farmer's markets allow for homemade products as well as raw goods. But there is a unique sales platform available for homemade products that don't usually apply to raw produce and raw goods. Craft and specialty fairs usually come around at specific times of the year, and it's the opportunity to set up a booth and sell your goods over the course of a few days. Specialty fairs, such as renaissance fairs, are additional opportunities. If you can make fishing lures or quilts, then you have a place in most specialty fairs that might come to your county.

Understanding Cottage Food Laws

Although initially it seems that cottage food laws are restrictive and troublesome, they are much more lenient than regulations that small business owners face. Cottage food laws allow people to sell homemade food to the public without going through extensive licensing. The primary focus is to understand the federal requirements and know which foods require labeling and which foods are outright banned. These laws vary from state to state.

But mostly, cottage food laws give an outline on which food needs to be refrigerated, how to process foods by canning, and other elements regarding spoilage. Some foods are not allowed to be produced in a home kitchen because they offer very specific health risks. However, with some permits or certain licensing, you may be able to sell these at farmer's markets or through similar platforms. Always be sure to research the cottage food laws in your state thoroughly.

Teaching and Experience Sharing

Chapter 11 will cover how to share your learning experiences, and how you can make your experience-sharing profitable. For now, we will go through the basics of teaching and experience-sharing as something you can make a profit from, and the many different ways to do it. You have the option of starting a blog or giving classes or even getting involved with local neighbors who want to learn how to homestead. The real element to consider here is that you shouldn't hesitate to charge for your time; even though you're not selling an outright product, you're selling a skill set.

Helping Others Learn Through Courses or Lessons

When just starting out, you should sit down and carefully set out what each lesson should accomplish. After you determine what each lesson will accomplish, you'll need to determine how you will communicate the information in each lesson and what activities or exercises you'll provide to help build that particular skill or bit of knowledge. What this is doing is writing a course plan and multiple lesson plans. You can find many different lesson plans online which can serve as examples.

If you do decide to give courses or lessons on homesteading, you need to think about the learning environment carefully. For example, if you're giving courses and charging money, your home kitchen may not be suitable; you may need to use a community kitchen or a commercial-grade kitchen because, in some counties, there are strict health-code requirements. When working or giving classes on your property, you may take greater steps to ensure that the grounds are safe and there is minimal risk of injury. Additionally, you may need to temporarily rent a commercial or commissary kitchen where you can host classes for kitchen activities in a food-safe environment.

Where to Sell

Getting into where exactly you can sell your goods can be a bit complex as local governments have varying laws and restrictions. By and large, you should expect to be able to sell the majority of your goods at a farmer's market. It may be a good idea to branch out and attend multiple farmer's markets, be they local or in more distant cities. However, if you look beyond farmers' markets, you'll have options to sell online, and you may open a small shop if it seems profitable, or you may sell out of your own home if you can manage it in your area.

Farmer's Markets – These markets are specifically for locally grown and produced items. Farmer's markets are legal, and on a federal level, the government sees them as a way to promote regional agriculture and assure a supply of fresh and local produce for residents. Typically, farmer's markets are restricted to small family farmers and homesteaders as they don't have the opportunities to sell in larger grocery chains. When setting up with the farmer's market, there are restrictions. You can't have a middleman, or a broker, involved; if a city tells you that it's required, then they're not conforming to federal law. There is the chance that a County agent or federal agent may visit your land to ensure that what you're selling at the market was grown or produced by you. Typically, farmer's markets will have a farmers' market committee that will have a combination of market growers and consumers that enforce rules and policies specific to that association.

Personal Online Shop - It can be difficult to get started, but in the long-run, it is usually easier to sell goods online than it is to run a small shop. A personal online shop will require a dedicated website and the use of an e-Commerce facilitator such as Shopify or Magento. Although it can seem complicated at first, with a consultant or a knowledgeable friend you can set up a website for less than a few hundred dollars in just a couple of hours. Websites are not as expensive as they used to be, and they're not as complicated to set up as most people believe. Once your online shop is set up, it is as easy as doing some simple maintenance to ensure that the products you have available are also available online for customers to view. You do need to be very careful with what you post online for sale, however, as there may be restrictions on cottage food laws and how you can ship certain items safely.

Online Crafting and Homemade Goods Platforms - Platforms such as Etsy, Aftcra, Artfire, Cratejoy, and Absolute Arts allow people to sell handmade products online. Using online crafting or homemade goods platforms can be a much easier way to get a jump start on selling goods online without having your own dedicated website. These platforms do take a small percentage of what you earn and may have additional fees based on shipping and other services.

Explore which platforms you would be interested in using and research their fees and user agreements carefully. For example, Etsy allows its sellers to sell food and edible items as long as they follow government regulations. Their Seller Handbook offers specific information on how to sell, ship, and package food items in ways that comply with federal government regulations.

Selling Out of Your Home – For home-based businesses, there's a handful of unique struggles. First, every county can set their own restrictions. Second, each county and state can have different permit requirements and, finally, you may be required to have certain insurance policies, such as liability insurance. When selling food or homemade products out of your home, you need to register as a business. Additionally, you'll need to go through your city, county, and state to determine if there are permits necessary for you to sell from your residence. For example in California, one of the most restrictive states, you will need to have one type of permit to sell directly from your home and at farmer's markets, and another permit if you plan on selling through those platforms and additional venues such as a local store or restaurant. And you'll be asked to provide information for all of your ingredients, your recipes, and where you're sourcing your ingredients, as well as having to make labels for each product you sell. This is why many homesteaders sell products directly from their front door. Your city or county may have a wide variety of exceptions available to you if you are only selling raw goods. For example, again within California, producers of raw unprocessed foods may only need a certified producer certificate rather than a handful of permits and regular check-ins from the public health inspector.

How to Build A Profitable Homestead

Whether you're still planning your homestead, or you've had a successful one for a few years, you can start with a basic checklist to make your homestead more profitable.

- What income streams can you access from your homestead (or homestead plans) without changing anything?
- What resources are available?

- Will you need additional resources?
- Define your customer (who do you ideally want to sell to?)
- Identify customer needs (e.g., they want organic options, they are trying to get away from big stores, etc.)
- How is your product different?
- How will you set your prices?
- Will you need an online presence or a community presence, or both?
- Write your business plan.

This checklist will help guide you through the process of establishing your options and eventually creating a homestead with opportunities for profit. It is important to make a business plan, even if you only continue forward as a cottage food operator, as that document will serve to help you make decisions and set goals.

On a final note, it is important to ensure that the purpose of self-sustainability within your homestead remains the top priority. If you're selling so much product that your homestead itself is withering, then you don't have a sustainable model, and you may need to scale back on your customer base or scale up your operations and become a larger business. Many homesteads are profitable in ways other than simply living off their properties. While you're still in the planning stages of putting your homestead together, it's a great time to explore how you might bring together homesteading, your hobbies, and the opportunity to bring more income into your household.

Chapter 9: 8 Resources to Consider

How and where can you start? Certainly, it's difficult to gather up the money necessary to purchase equipment, seeds, chickens, and the materials necessary to build a coop and garden boxes. But you can do it. There are many resources available to help you get started; some are financially based, while others help you build experience and skills.

There are four key elements you want to cover when you're looking for high-quality resources. First, traveling and labor assistance. Although you're not moving heavy equipment, you might be creating a lot of garden boxes, building a chicken coop, or planting trees; these aren't tasks that one person can happily do on their own. The more help you have, the more likely it is that you can develop diverse skills. The laborers that you'll find through volunteer systems may have no experience, or this may be their retired hobby with decades of experience. Always accept help happily.

Second, you need support from your county or possibly your city. Some cities, but nearly all counties, have restrictions on what you can do in your own backyard. It might seem outrageous that any government office within U.S. could say what you can or can't do on your own land. However, there are some very reasonable explanations for why you can't dig in certain areas, build in others, or even have chickens. For example, chickens are noisy, and if your city has a restriction on noise within your neighborhoods because of other residents, it may mean that chickens aren't an available option. You may not be able to dig lines for waterways or water systems because of buried gas or power lines. These obstacles may or may not be present within your neighborhood. You must communicate with your city or county and acquire any necessary permits.

Third, you need to find exemptions for farms, property tax credits, and other tax elements. If you profit or earn some type of income from your land, then you may need to calculate your income and pay taxes on that revenue. And if you give back to the community, you may have access to some tax breaks or write-offs. If your homestead becomes your business, you may have the ability to write off certain pieces of equipment. It's best to find the resources you need to figure out what may or may not be available to you. When it comes to taxes and money management, nothing compares to a Certified Public Accountant. Although you may have the skillset and resources to handle your finances on your own, always keep an open mind toward hiring a CPA if you grow or start earning significant income from your homestead.

Finally, there's the 'where to start' resources. Although this guide is very comprehensive, it might be helpful to have a few local resources available when you need a bit more guidance. Besides getting local help in getting started, you can find the support you need through these trying times within the homesteading community. These resources are more for emotional support, for someone to step in and say, "Yes, you can do it."

Let's dive into the resources and keep in mind that some are very up to date with information on modern techniques and implementing modern systems, while other resources here only refer to traditional methods or support "traditional" homesteaders. It's vital that you cast a wide net, as it can take a while to find the right resources for your mini-farm.

Finding Help with Labor and Developing a Skill Set

The Worldwide Opportunities on Organic Farms or WWOOF, helps new farmers connect with local volunteers. These volunteers can greatly vary in experience, but often you'll exchange education and culture while working with this group. You may find that many people within your community are happy to jump in on a project and literally roll up their sleeves.

Volunteers with WWOOF will usually live with the host for a short time, and it allows them to experience life as a farmer. For you, that may mean visitors in your home that genuinely want to connect with your land and support a change in how we view and cultivate our food.

So, you would sign up with WWOOF as a host, and then essentially place an ad that will be put up onto the site where volunteers could see it. They respond through the site, and then WWOOF contacts you. It's not like Craigslist, where just anyone can contact you or view your information. WWOOF likes to urge people to give it a try and ensures that the process is as safe as possible. All volunteers go through an extensive application process, and not everyone enters the program. Additionally, most complaints will result in an immediate suspension, if not a permanent termination, of their membership. You can always do thorough interviews before accepting a WWOOF candidate.

Another way to find like-minded people that support local farms is through your local 4-H chapter or FFA groups. Although they are often much younger, you can collaborate with the group leaders to contribute to your community and future farmers or agricultural enthusiasts while supporting your local chapter.

For help through your immediate community, you might also explore your local community center. Often these centers can help like-minded adults come together. Keep in mind that if you get involved in these types of communities, they often expect you to give back. For example, you may plan part of a 4-H project with your mini-farm and continue working as an adult volunteer within the organization.

Assistance from U.S. Department of Agriculture and NIFA

The Cooperative Extension Office offers help with local and individual assistance for everything involving research, practical application, and more. The National Institute of Food and Agriculture has long led the way for researching agriculture in America. That means that they look at different methods of development, land cultivation, and other things that lead to a plentiful harvest. While working with the United States Department of Agriculture, these two authorities created the Cooperative Extension System. The System serves to translate the research of the National Institute of Food and Agriculture, with practical applications that farmers and ranchers on all scales can put to use.

You can access information and find out what monetary or informational support is available in your area by contacting the CES (Cooperative Extension System) office in your county. They provide not only access to grants and funding awards, but also education. Although there are no formal education credits that you can earn through CES, you can obtain valuable information from these groups. They have operated for over 100 years and help families, communities, farmers, and ranchers build sustainable systems within their homesteads, community gardens, and more.

Grants and Funding

When you look at the full costs of building a homestead, even in your backyard, you're looking at a few thousand dollars. The average startup costs over the first two years are about $5,000. Most of those costs happen in the first few months as you build a chicken coop, purchase seeds, obtain storing materials or equipment, and buy chickens. Now, those costs are on top of all your current bills, because you're not saving on groceries or products you can cultivate at home yet. Most people, even those living paycheck to paycheck, can make $5,000 happen over the course of two years. But there are many avenues to help you obtain funding for the initial investments. Grants and other forms of funding are usually available to help cover or entirely cover startup costs that otherwise might dissuade you from starting your homestead.

Grants.gov offers support in small farm grants, particularly if you're looking to buy land and equipment. The USDA, or United States Department of Agriculture, also provides specialized grants and small loans. For example, if taking out a loan to get your mini farm started now is part of your plan, then you need to look to find the best possible loan repayment options. An FSA loan would allow you to use the loan for buying land, equipment, livestock, supplies, seeds, and feed. There are also rural development loan and grant assistance programs that can help with things like setting up community facilities and utilities. Finally, there is the opportunity to enter into the United States Department of Agriculture Farm Service Agency for Beginning Farmers and Ranchers. This program contributes a substantial portion of support for guaranteed farm ownership through operating loan funds directly to beginning farmers and ranchers. There aren't restrictions based on how much property you have available, so you can apply while still using a backyard for your homestead.

Sustainable Agriculture Research and Education provides lists of grants that usually stem from community relationships or educational institutions.

Resources for Information on Sustainable Agriculture

When it comes to finding information on sustainable agriculture, it's easy to get lost in the sea of information, or misinformation. While this book provides a guide, we can't possibly cover every possible stumbling block through your first few years in backyard homesteading. However, we can help you find resources that have brought together years and years of research and studies so you can access reliable information quickly. The USDA Alternative Farming Systems Information Center is among the leaders in providing information on sustainable food systems in agriculture. They're recognized as the primary authority on all things related to sustainable agriculture from aquaculture to community farming support. They're a great resource, but it can be a bit difficult to navigate their website. If you're looking to use their information often, you might index or bookmark your most frequented pages on your phone or in your Internet browser.

Beginningfarmers.org is another primary resource for, you guessed it, beginning farmers. The aptly-named website is up to date with the most recent developments in small farming and agriculture. It's a great place to find news updates and get answers to questions for things such as emergency relief, or where to find a beginners training course for your area. They also have a forum for helping people find farm jobs and internships. If you're willing to pay for labor, it's a great place to post an open position and find people genuinely interested in farming and agriculture.

The USDA website has a lot of tutorials for small-scale farming. It's a great place to start on reliable DIY videos that you can follow easily. With the USDA video library, with everything from the National Agricultural Library, you can find tons of videos on remaining organic and other elements that involve expanding your mini-farm, such as aquaponics.

When you're working with agriculture, it's important to know which resources are credible and fit your style of farming. With these resources, you should have no problem finding any information you need. You can return to any of these resources again and again. What's important is that you understand that there are so many resources available. All too often, people make homesteading feel like an isolated existence. But clearly, there are many communities and many sectors of the government that offer support to individuals. As you start homesteading, keep in mind that you're not alone. Know that if you need help, you can get help, and you can probably get it pretty easily. Keep tabs for these resources as you plan out how you will start your homestead. Don't be afraid to apply for grants or funding simply because you're homesteading in your backyard. Also, don't be afraid to watch video tutorials or read the information that is more relative to large homesteads but is something that you might be able to scale down.

Chapter 10: Care and Maintenance

Care and ongoing maintenance are mandatory. You must always be thinking about and preparing for the next season. That means tending to gardens, rotating livestock, and maintaining your structures. You must consider your climate and weather conditions with high regard.

Homesteading is a process that is always on, and that means that regardless of the weather or even if you're sick, certain things have to get done to maintain your current level of success. As you're still in the planning phase of homesteading, you can take greater care now to develop a low maintenance homestead. When you have fewer demands on maintenance, you can devote your time to more productive tasks.

Caring for Gardens

When it comes to garden maintenance, you'll need to worry about weeding, mulching, and fertilizing. Weeding is very straightforward. If you see anything growing in your garden that is unwanted, pull it up. But the best way to ensure low-maintenance weeding is by properly mulching. Mulching is using a material to cover the soil to prevent weed growth and slow down water loss. Organic options include straw, grass clippings, leaves, and newspapers. However, many people choose to use bark or wood chips that have a chemical treatment.

Fertilizing certainly contributes to overall plant health, but as a maintenance measure, it promotes good soil health. Most plants, when properly cared for, won't last more than two years. While it is important to take care of the plant, it is also important to care for the soil. For fertilizing, you can use organic options such as liquid seaweed, alfalfa meal, hummus, and compost. For non-organic options, you can use any fertilizer available at local home improvement stores.

When it comes to the winter months, you'll want to ensure that you have protection for your plants. If you live in an area where the ground freezes through, you might consider using a heating wire. Additionally, if you live in an area where there are harsh summers, you should consider using shades or awnings to protect your plants during the harshest days.

Upkeep on Structures and Equipment

The maintenance of your structures and equipment is pretty straightforward. You want to create a calendar that will help you identify minor repairs before they become major problems. Any structure on your property with a roof should be inspected every six months, including the roof on your chicken coop or goat pens. It is much easier to replace a shingle than to replace the roof on anything. Additionally, every three to six months, you should walk around each structure on your property and evaluate the sides and the foundation for possible damage. You can schedule repairs during seasons where repairs may be cheaper. For example, many contractors are willing to do minor foundational repairs or wall repairs for outdoor structures in the spring or the fall at cheaper rates because there aren't harsh working conditions.

When it comes to your equipment, you'll want to work with a smaller time frame. If you have a tractor, you'll want to have it serviced every three months and use that service schedule to evaluate it for needed repairs as well. If you have additional specialty equipment, such as a wind generator or solar panels, then you'll need to explore the specific demands of upkeep for that equipment. Solar panel upkeep, for example, varies by brand, and you may need to clean them daily or use a once-a-month chemical treatment to keep them clean.

Maintenance for Livestock

Although you might feel bad when you kill a plant, livestock is a little more concerning. You want to ensure that all of your livestock has a clean living environment, but you also want to make that environment easy to maintain. You can create a low maintenance livestock plan, and doing that should naturally result in a cleaner living environment and better living conditions for your animals. It is exceptionally difficult with livestock because if one gets sick, it is common that all the rest in the flock or the herd will become sick as well. Through careful planning and maintenance, you can avoid losing an entire flock or losing an animal due to poor conditions.

Chickens

Generally, chickens are very easy to take care of. Although some do like human contact, most aren't bothered if you can't spend very much time with them. Additionally, with a feeder and access to water, they don't need very much at all. You do need to collect their eggs almost daily, but that is more for food safety. So, what should you plan for when it comes to chicken maintenance?

To create a low maintenance chicken coop, you can make the demand for cleaning much easier to manage. Chickens create a lot of waste. It can be a hassle to go through and clear out the chicken waste once a week when in that one week, it can almost cement to the floor of the chicken coop. Instead, use a linoleum floor that you can spray off with a power spray nozzle, and then add chicken litter on top of it.

There is a technique called deep litter method, which is used to create compost beneath a tall layer of litter. What happens is that you allow anything left on the floor to compost, and you add litter on top, and this makes for one really big cleaning job every few months. It really comes down to your preference in your time management, whether you would be better off cleaning it out once a week with linoleum floor or doing it once every few months with the deep litter method.

Another element of maintenance for chickens to consider is stress. These birds are very prone to stress, and when they are stressed, they stop laying eggs. One of the biggest factors that can lead to stress and molting is a poor diet. The chickens are omnivores, and they require a lot of vitamins and protein, so chicken feed alone won't be enough. Instead, you can provide them with crushed eggshells, oyster shells, and ensure that they have a chicken run where they can forage for insects. It is much easier to integrate these elements into part of the regular diet than trying to correct sickness or molting from stress every time malnutrition becomes an issue.

When it comes to maintenance for chickens, you do need to plan for what will happen when your hens stop laying eggs. When hens stop laying eggs because of their age, you'll need to choose between allowing them to live out their days in retirement in the coop or throughout the yard or to process them. It seems worth mentioning that older hens don't make for very good meat production and processing them doesn't usually yield much meat that's worth using.

Finally, you'll need to plan for extreme weather conditions, and that includes hot and cold weather. Because your chickens have a coop, they have an indoor area to go to, use that indoor area to build in extremely cold weather measures. Emergency preparedness can include heat lamps that you can plug in or switch on only when necessary. When it comes to hot temperatures, you might want to ensure that there is not only enough natural shade but that there is some type of additional cooling unit. Many homesteaders will freeze large containers or bottles with water overnight and then put them into the shaded portion of the coop or the run underneath the coop in the hottest part of the day.

Goats and Sheep

Goats and sheep usually prefer to have a pen even if they don't use it all the time. Having a pan with a windbreak and a roof can make the winter and summer seasons much easier on these animals. You'll also want to ensure that they always have access to drinkable water, and if you live in a climate where water will freeze through in pipes, you may need a small heater for their water container. It's also important to ensure that they always have access to food, but for emergency preparedness, they need double what they typically eat throughout the wintertime.

With both goats and sheep, you'll want to have fencing around a very specific pasture, and that pasture should not have all of your livestock together. Goats and sheep can live together fairly peacefully. However, neither of these should be mixed with your cow pasture. Ensure that your pasture has some sunny spots and a shaded area.

There is a special note with goats that doesn't apply to sheep. Goats are destructive. Given any opportunity, goats will go into an area of the land or even your home where they should not be and destroy virtually anything they can. What you need for your fencing is a woven wire or "no-climb" horse fencing that is at least four feet high. Remember that goats are excellent climbers and can jump fairly high, so keep any structures within the pasture well away from the fence line. Putting in and upkeeping this fence is part maintenance and part prevention in order to avoid having to do more maintenance than necessary.

The good news about these destructive qualities is that they turn the ground better than most professional equipment can manage. You should plan, as part of your maintenance calendar, to rotate your goat pasture every after every-other crop rotation.

Cows

It might initially seem that cows are low maintenance animals, but that's not quite the case. Cows, in addition to their food and water, need salt and minerals in the form of licks, they also need to have a spacious pasture. It's also important as part of your maintenance that you spend time with the cows to reduce possible aggressive behavior. Cows are not inherently aggressive, but they are very large animals, and if they get scared or feel threatened, they can do a lot of damage to your property and cause severe injuries as well.

Cattle certainly need shelter, but it doesn't have to be over the top. If you have a wind wall and a roof, or a 3-sided structure, then that is enough for them to seek shelter during poor weather.

Cows do need trimming, and you should schedule a visit with your veterinarian every six months. The veterinarian can come to your property and conduct any trimming necessary, and they can also address any infection that may have taken root in their hooves. Additionally, cows need to be vaccinated regularly for rabies and a wide variety of other contagious diseases. Some of the vaccines will vary by region, so it's important that you discuss these vaccines and a vaccine schedule with your veterinarian.

How to Make Your Homestead as Low Maintenance as Possible

The best thing to do with maintenance is to make it as systematic as possible. That means relying heavily on automated systems and a calendar. For example, with your livestock, you may have a standing appointment with your veterinarian every six months. Having that recurring appointment takes away the stress of having to call and schedule an appointment every time you think that your cow or goat might have a hoof problem.

Low maintenance gardens are often seasonal. A seasonal garden allows you to put fresh mulch and liven up the soil between seasons; however, it does deplete the lifespan of your plants. You can also make your gardens low maintenance by implementing a watering system that will save you from watering them by hand.

Finally, use any resources that you can to ensure that cleaning up the livestock environment is as easy as possible for chickens that can be using linoleum flooring instead of wood. For cows, it can mean having their compost pile right near their pasture, so it is easy to add that manure to the pile. You might also invest in equipment that makes it easier to pick up and transport manure.

Make a Homestead Maintenance Calendar

Over the years, and as you develop your homestead, your homestead maintenance calendar will take shape. For now, you can start with a basic calendar that lays out what you should be doing from month to month. Then after your first-year homestead year, you can look back at the calendar and see what did or did not work out well for you. Every homestead is unique, and your environment and weather conditions will drastically change what your maintenance calendar will look like. However, a starter calendar might look like this:

- **January**
  - Make goals
  - Calculate expenses from last year
  - Sow indoor seeds
  - Clean and disinfect chicken feeders and waterers
  - Ensure all heat lamps are working
- **February**
  - Design spring vegetable garden
  - Tap trees
  - Prune orchards
  - Sow indoor seeds for spring garden
  - Harvest end of winter garden
  - Clean out any pasture area
- **March**
  - Sow indoor seeds for late spring – peppers, tomatoes
  - Change chicken bedding and clean nesting boxes
  - Purchase feeder pigs or make livestock purchase of goats/sheep
  - Maintenance check on roofing and structures
- **April**
  - Plant perennial beds – prepare with heavy compost week before planting
  - Early vegetables

o Start spring compost heap

o Change chicken bedding and clean. Nesting boxes

o Clean and disinfect chicken feeders and waterers

o Install screens

- **May**

o Plant annuals

o Plant late-spring vegetables

o Clean out any pasture area

o Introduce new chickens

- **June**

o Start haying for the winter supply

o Change chicken bedding and clean nesting boxes

o Harvest and preserve berries

o Harvest early-spring produce – freeze vegetables

o Sow for early fall crops

- **July**

o Clean and disinfect chicken feeders and waterers

o Canning

o Freeze or pickle half of harvest

o Late haying

o The seed for late fall crops

o Mulch garden

- **August**

o Change chicken bedding and clean nesting boxes

o Butcher broiler chickens

o Freeze or can orchard harvest

o Harvest corn, wheat crops

- **September**

o Maintenance check on roofing and structures

o Clean and disinfect chicken feeders and waterers

o Preserve tomatoes

o Mulch garden

- **October**

o Gather firewood

- Can applesauce
- Can pumpkin butter
- Winterize perennial garden
- Heavy mulch all gardens
- Change chicken bedding and clean nesting boxes
- Put up and check all heat lamps
- **November**
  - Freezer baking
  - Butcher second round broiler chickens
  - Mulch winter beds
  - Manage winter garden
- **December**
  - Update maintenance calendar for the upcoming year
  - Estimated taxes
  - Butcher cow, pig, sheep, or goat
  - Check pipes and waterers for freezing

Maintenance can be rather easy if you plan well but there is really no telling what lies in store for your first year. Using a generic calendar like this one where you simply remove any tasks that don't apply to you is a great place to start. However, you may need to make adjustments as you go. It can also be difficult to start maintenance as you're still developing your homestead and making your homestead plan. Unfortunately, maintenance is hard to catch-up on. So, if your garden is up first, then start your garden maintenance the very next month. Then start maintenance on your chicken coop the month after your chickens get moved in. Then start maintenance on your harvest when your first harvest comes around. That can help you build a maintenance calendar while you're still setting up your homestead, and it can make maintenance down the road much easier.

Chapter 11: Sharing Your Learning Experience

One of the unique things that come with homesteading is the ability to share your experience. Although you are far from being the only homesteader around, the challenges that you face may not be the same challenges that others have experienced already. By sharing your experiences, you can help others better prepare for changes in seasons, issues with crops and animals, and much more. However, it's not just about giving back to the homesteading community. You can even create another avenue of income by sharing your experiences.

Through blogs and community events, you can become a teacher in your own right. We'll explore each way that you can share your experiences, and the benefits and possible revenue that could come with each option. If you decide to share your homestead experience through a blog or events within your community, you'll need to consider the skill set you already have and your ability to market yourself and your homesteading brand.

Vlogs

Vlogging or video logging is the method of recording your experiences and posting them online in a video format. Typically, the people that are doing this are just called YouTubers because YouTube is the most popular platform at the moment. However, people were creating video diaries and recording certain aspects of their life long before YouTube existed.

Don't get stuck asking yourself if you can be a YouTuber. Instead, ask yourself if you can approach documenting your life at an almost nonstop pace.

To start a vlog, you should consider a few of the main elements. For example, because of YouTube's presence, you will likely need a YouTube channel. However, to reach other audiences, you might also consider having a website. In addition to a website, you may reach out to followers, fans, or people searching for content through social media platforms such as Instagram. One of the major mistakes that people new to vlogging make is that they pigeonhole themselves into one platform. Then when another platform takes off and gains attention, they can't pivot in time to keep up with all the changes.

Essential Elements of a Vlog
- High-quality documentary-style videos
- The ability to present yourself in front of the camera well
- Basic video editing skills
- Recording equipment
- Time to dedicate to posting and maintaining your channel

Now, you don't need to start out with all of these things. In fact, many people start by recording videos on their phones or learning to video edit as they go. There's no need to rush out and spend thousands on video recording equipment if you're not even sure if it will work for you. Basically, if you're not passionate about it, don't worry about it. Vlogging can turn some people away from their passions, such as homesteading. It's common for "YouTubers" to experience burn-out after a few years and then completely abandon the things that they wanted to share on their channel.

When it comes to revenue, there is a lot of opportunity with vlogging, if you're willing to put in the work. You probably won't become an overnight celebrity sensation that regularly receives tens of thousands of dollars in advertising revenue from YouTube. However, you might be able to create a nice supplementary income. It's important to note that vlogging does not generally turn out as a consistent income. While top earners on YouTube make upwards of $10 million annually, you shouldn't expect to hit those numbers. In fact, when Learning Hub sat down and averaged out the views per monetized video, you'd need about 1,000 views on any particular video to earn less than ten dollars. Technically, the advertisers working through YouTube's monetization system payout $0.18 per view or $18 for 1,000 views but Google, the ad aggregate for the platform keeps 45% of that revenue as a type of finder's fee —leaving the vloggers with only $9.90 per 1,000 views. There are other elements to consider, and advertising through YouTube's monetization system is not the only way to make money as a vlogger. Some of YouTube's top influencers or personalities don't use YouTube's monetization system because they don't want to interrupt their viewers with ads. Instead, they may align their personal brand with a sponsor or work with other local brands to advertise in a non-invasive way. A lot of people who craft, homestead, or do other lifestyle-esque videos will choose to do this as it allows them to give information and valuable input on brands and products within the industry.

So, what happens if you don't want ads, and you don't want sponsors? Well, you can still use vlogging as a platform to share your experiences without it producing an income. Or, you can create your own merchandise that promotes your brand. You can also add in a system such as Patreon, where you can ask subscribers to pay a membership fee to access additional or premium content in addition to what you already post. Often vloggers that do this will create fun and entertaining videos for free, then use Patreon or a similar platform to provide tutorials, how-to videos, and more. When doing this, you'll need a bit more tech for proper execution. You may need a mailing list and website to make sure that your premium subscribers get all the additional content that you promised.

Is it worth it? For many people, the act of vlogging is relaxing and cathartic. It's a creative outlet to share this monumental change in your life. Most people haven't grown up homesteading, and it's probably safe to say that even the experienced can have unexpected situations, and such things crop up as they build their homestead. If you start your vlog channel as you build your homestead, or even during the planning process, you're cataloging or recording your experience not just for others but for yourself as well. This is a unique way to share your experiences and get involved in a community that you may not have known even existed.

Blogs

Blogging is exactly like vlogging, but instead of using a video format, you deliver written content. If you love to write or journal, then blogging is an excellent way to document and share your homesteading experience. Typically, through blogging, you'll post to one platform, and it will read as a blend of an article and journal-style entry. It really won't read like a news story or an article that you might read on social media platforms; it should be more conversational in structure. Many people write their blogs as though they're talking to a close friend. That allows the language to be a bit more flexible and stray from rigid structures that you might expect to see in most textbooks or guides.

It is important to note that you don't need to be an all-star writer to have a blog. In fact, while having a general grasp of grammar is always good, a lot of blogging breaks standard rules for writing. Because it's a conversational tone in approach, blogging is a lot more forgiving with writing fundamentals than starting a novel or writing a weekly news article. If your first instinct is, "I can't write, so I can't write a blog," then give yourself a little credit and try anyway.

A few of the blogs that stand out among homesteaders are The Self-Sufficient Homeacre and The Homestead Survival. They use two very different approaches to blogging in tone and style. They also have different scopes on what they share regarding homesteading.

Looking at The Self-Sufficient Homeacre, a lot of the articles have to do with growing plants, raising chickens, preserving the harvest, and cooking. It's a pretty typical look at homesteading. One article entitled, "How to Grow Food in Small Spaces" delivers an onslaught of options for growing plants when you're tight on space. The tone is fairly direct but still friendly, and the website itself is fairly "clean" but does contain a few posted ads and then affiliate ads.

The Homestead Survival has too many ads, and the webpage or blog looks pretty cluttered. However, everything is organized and has a place, and is generally easy to navigate. What they have done here is create many smaller options to access sections of their website which address different needs. You're not scrolling through endless articles that flit from one topic to another. This blog delivers household tips, DIY projects, home remedies, food storage and canning tips, and even knife skills for those who raise animals for meat. The Homestead Survival is a drastic contrast to the other blog, and the tone is a lot more personal. They are transparent about their numbers in terms of what they spend and what they earn, and whether a DIY is cheaper than buying something pre-made.

The point in comparing these two blogs is to show that the content itself can vary drastically. Both listed here are homesteading blogs; both generate revenue for their website owners. However, it's important to know exactly what you want to deliver through your homesteading blog. A lot of time and dedication goes into creating and then maintaining a blog, so if you're not confident in handling daily tasks that may or may not generate revenue, blogging may not be right for you.

To Start a Blog, You Will Need:
- Website or platform such as Tumblr
- Plenty of content – It's best to start a blog with at least 50 articles ready to publish.

- Time to continue writing articles to support your blog; consistent posting is key!
- The domain name and web host (which can quickly become expensive)
- Strong social media presence

Unlike using a video platform such as YouTube, you don't have access to a giant base of people. You'll need to pull traffic to your site. To generate traffic to your site with the hope of someone clicking an ad or purchasing an affiliate product, you will need to have a really strong social media presence. You may very well end up blogging and vlogging to generate the necessary income that you expected from sharing your experiences.

Many people choose to blog, however, without ads or without demanding an income from this creative outlet. If you're looking for a way to reach the homesteading community, a blog is a good option. Not everything that you do at home needs to generate an income. However, there are ways to provide an ad-free user experience or to use a free platform that you can't monetize and still profit from your blog. Going back to Patreon, you can market premier content, merchandise, and even one-on-one lessons while still hosting a free blog that serves as a creative outlet for you.

Hosting Community Events and Getting Involved

Hosting a community event is a huge deal. Fortunately, a lot of the soft skills that you've developed through setting up a homestead will pay off here. All that work you put into planning the homestead will feel pretty familiar when you're planning your community event. You may request permission from your city to host an event for your neighborhood or host a private event with a limited capacity. Each option has different requirements when it comes to permits and planning, so it's worth the effort to decide before you even start just how big your event should be. It's always best to start small and work your way up. There is no need to have a citywide event if you don't know the extent of interest within your community.

Private Event with Set Capacity

Now, in theory, you could host a private event at your house and not have to request any permission from your local government. It would be about the same as having a barbeque over the weekend. However, if you're going to be selling goods, providing food, or taking up a substantial amount of street parking, it's better to alert the city of your plans than to face a possible ticket later.

As you plan a private event, you'll need to put a cap on how many people can attend. You could always start with a shortlist of people you would like to invite and ask them if there is anyone that they would like to bring, or leave it open on your invitation list with a plus-one for each person. Hosting private events like this are a good way to get a feel for how many people are interested in homesteading. People like your siblings or close friends might show up just to support you, but it can still be a fun and informative experience for them and whoever they bring with them.

When you do a private event, you might want to focus on one primary element of homesteading. To cover all of homesteading in just an hour or two would be overwhelming for you and your attendees. However, if you do a private event on herb gardening, you can better control the conversation and keep people engaged rather than jumping from herb gardening to canning to raising chickens.

Keep in mind that when you host a private event, it's always best to do everything that a host should do. That means make sure that parking is available, having food or some type of snacks available as well as beverages. Make your guests comfortable, and it can be a great experience for everyone involved.

Neighborhood Events

Neighborhood events can be really fun, and they can become a monthly or an annual event. If your neighborhood doesn't currently do block parties, then you might not know where to start. First, canvas your neighborhood and find out how many people are interested. By this point, it might already be well known that your lemon tree is the best place to get lemons in town. So why would your neighbors miss the chance to talk to you about home-growing plants and the differences between what you produce at home and what you find at the grocery store?

When you're implementing a neighborhood event, you should expect a lot more people than you might have at a private event. This gives you a little more opportunity to address different elements of homesteading and cover a broader range of topics than just the one thing people wanted to talk about. When planning a neighborhood event, you should collaborate with other neighbors as well as the city to ensure that you have permits for everything and that there are enough activities and information centers for everyone to be entertained.

One of the more important elements that you need to express when you're doing a neighborhood event is that you're available to help people that want to get started. Sharing your experiences is the first step in helping other people understand and maybe begin homesteading. Ultimately, when you're sharing your experience in a face-to-face situation, you should be open to getting much more involved.

Volunteering Through Community Outlets

Community outlets such as 4-H clubs or the Future Farmers of America are a great way to get involved. These groups and other similar groups connect adults with a certain skill set with teens and children who aim to develop those skills. As a homesteader, your ability to share your experiences can help others cultivate a skill set for building self-sustainability within their lifestyle. Being an active participant in these communities allows for the sharing of your experiences, but it also allows you to engage on a deeper level.

You're not just teaching children how chicks are hatched. You're teaching them about the natural life cycle. You're teaching them about the importance of what chickens do for our world. For many, it's an uplifting way to share your experiences because you're going beyond what just happens on your mini-farm, and you're expanding that to show how people can create the experience that you've had and build something for themselves, too.

Getting involved with community outlets is fairly easy. You can reach out to local chapters of well-established clubs that we mentioned above, or you can contact the city and your school district. Even if your city doesn't have a local 4-H club, it's likely that some of the high schools in your area do have agricultural classes. Because of how the school system has changed, many people in those classes don't have access to an actual garden. It's all theory learning. But by volunteering your experiences and possibly your homestead for a short time, you can connect with teens or young adults who are looking for ways to develop their skill set.

Sharing Through Storytelling

Now that you have an idea of the different methods for sharing your experience, you might wonder what comes next. What stories do you have to tell? Is homesteading too boring to share with others? Is it too much like what everyone else is already doing?

One of the reasons why we touched on two of the most popular blogs in the homesteading world is to show their differences. Open up any two homesteading vlogs on YouTube and you'll get drastically different accounts of homesteading, because everyone's experiences are unique. You may have suffered from the same cold snap as a fellow homesteader in your area, but there's no way that you and that person experienced it in the same way, responded in the same way, or came up against the same hardships with your plants and animals.

One of the best ways to start sharing your experiences, no matter your platform, is to use storytelling. Storytelling is something we do naturally and is a great way too not only teach but identify with people that you're sharing an experience with. For example, you can set out a list and say in the event of a hard freeze, you can do X, Y, and Z to sustain your crops. However, that doesn't communicate your experience. Through storytelling, you can say something like this:

"Winter came in, but I wasn't too worried, because it was the desert. My homesteading experiences would be harshest in the summer when I had to worry about keeping everything alive in the heat. But, when winter came, I realized that the desert gets exceptionally cold. I wasn't prepared with firewood or extra batteries, and I hadn't planned on things like heating lamps at all. After the first night, my chickens were in a sour state after having gone all night without water, and my poor herb garden was frozen. I went out the next day, get a small water heater for my chicken's water, and laid down some electric heat cable through the part of my garden that survived that first brutal night."

Simply put, posting a list or a how-to doesn't really help the community or help you explore your experiences from a reflective standpoint the way that storytelling does.

When sharing your experiences, keep in mind that people are listening, they're interested, and that you have something important to share. Your experiences can help others build better homesteads or even encourage them to try living a more self-sustaining life on their own. It's something that every homesteader should consider doing because of how much sharing your experience can contribute to the homesteading community. It can also offer quite a bit of relief on your part. You can look back and see what seemed like a monumental struggle at the time, and now in retrospect, it seems simple. You realize it was something important that you needed to learn and drastically changed your system for homesteading. Sharing most of your experiences can help others better prepare and give insight into your unique solutions to various homesteading challenges.

Chapter 12: Expanding Your Homestead

There are very few homesteaders that remain happy doing just the basic maintenance and upkeep on their land. Most have that drive to continue developing and cultivating new skills. Don't be surprised if, after a first year or two, when everything seems easy, you find yourself wanting to add something into your homesteading mix.

Fortunately, there is a vast array of homesteading specialties that you can add to your land. Some of these specialties don't necessarily fit the modern backyard homestead model, but if you have extra space, there's no reason you can't explore all of these more advanced homesteading activities.

Expanding into Cattle, Goats, Sheep, Pigs and Working Dogs

Raising livestock is difficult and you need to carefully consider how and when you will introduce them. Typically, goats and sheep need little room at all. Goats on their own don't need much space, but they can get destructive when they don't have enough room to move around.

You want to be sure that you have any necessary structure and pasture ready before you purchase any more livestock. When you expand into livestock, you have a few options about how they will contribute to your homestead. Cattle, goats, sheep, pigs, and even rabbits can all contribute to the homestead's meat supply. Additionally, cattle and goats are excellent for milk production. If you want to raise livestock, you can also explore options for herd-sharing and stud services to have your livestock bring in a profit.

If you're going to be adding livestock to your homestead, you should seriously consider bringing in a working dog as well. While it is always nice to have a dog around the house, a working dog's top priority won't be friendship. Well raised working dogs will have a constant need to be close to their herd, and they serve as a form of protection and stress relief. Cattle, goats, and sheep can all benefit from a working dog. A working dog can help the herd focus. It can keep them company, it can make them feel a sense of security, and it can alert you if anything is wrong at any time of day or night.

Some of the best breeds of working dogs include the Bernese mountain dog, Great Dane, German shepherds, Australian shepherds, and bloodhounds. These breeds are all athletic and should, with proper training, get along with nearly all other animals. Additionally, most of these breeds don't have a problem attacking larger pests such as raccoons or opossums that may bother your herd.

Beekeeping

As a homesteader, adding bees to your property can ensure that you always have a natural sweetener at home. And the bees can help pollinate your gardens, meaning larger yields. There really is no downside to beekeeping except maybe the occasional sting. To get started, you should reach out to your local beekeeping organizations and learn how bees use their hive. You'll want to have their hive and all of your necessary materials on hand before you get the bees on your property. It is always best to start your hive in the spring so that your bees can immediately get to work.

But you'll also have to learn how to harvest the honey, keep their hive clean, and store honey properly. Beekeeping can open a lot of doors in terms of creating products using beeswax and using home-gathered honey in your cooking. Bees don't require a lot of space, and you don't need a large hive, so you can start beekeeping with only a small amount of space.

Aquaponics

Aquaponics is a combination of gardening fish and vegetables together. Fish produce waste that feeds microbes, and then those microbes feed the plants with nutrients, and then the water gets filtered by the plants and returns to the fish. It is a complex system and does require quite a bit of careful planning. Additionally, you'll have to maintain the water constantly to ensure that your fish are healthy, and your plants are safe. But the payoff is that you can have more nutrient-rich vegetables and the availability of fish right in your backyard.

To get started with aquaponics, you might consider just having a fishpond. Then you can begin the introduction of aquaponics with controlled steps. The fish in a fishpond do need some care, but generally, they are self-sustaining. You may need a pump to keep the pond clean, and you may need to feed the fish regularly.

Hydroponics

What if that garage or shed you don't use could convert into more garden space? Hydroponics is the way to grow plants without soil. Typically, with hydroponics, plants will grow faster and offer bigger yields. Additionally, you can save a lot of space because instead of relying on nutrient-dense soil, you're giving the plants oxygenated nutrient-rich water.

Although hydroponics requires a lot of research to understand and implement, the basic approach is to keep plants' roots wet with nutrient-dense water solutions. You'll also want to ensure that you're providing the proper type of lighting for the plants that you're growing. Most plants that you would have in a garden require direct or partial indirect sunlight. So, in addition to having the hydroponic system set up, if your hydroponics garden is indoors you'll also need a full-scale lighting system.

Vertical Gardens

Have you run out of space but not great ideas for vegetables to plant? It is possible to grow vertical gardens where the plants are set into a pot that hangs off the side of the wall. You can mount vertical gardens on the side of your home, shed, or even your chicken coop. Some people worry about the extent of water damage that could happen to the side of their home or shed, but you can always protect against that with a bit of planning.

These vertical gardens are grabbing a ton of attention because of how simple they are to make. Just be sure that you have the time to care for them.

Expanding Your Homestead

It's amazing how much starting a homestead can boost your confidence in your ability to develop new skills and try new things. You may try a wide variety of expansions to your homestead, such as growing an herb garden or exploring different methods of plant cultivation. Expanding your homestead doesn't always call for more space. Always remember to be creative and use the resources that you have available. Homesteaders are often experts at finding new creative solutions to achieve their goals. Celebrate your homesteading anniversary by setting new goals and planning to build new skills!

Conclusion

Homesteading is a rewarding experience. You have learned how to plan throughout the year, accommodating different seasons, and living off the land. You will also face challenges that may demand you improve your skills and abilities. Homesteading is about self-sustainability while still devoting yourself to cultivating the land you have available to you. It is the opportunity to learn how to live simply while developing skills and your personality in a way that probably never seemed possible in our technological age.

Use the methods for planning, preparing, growing, and nurturing in this book to help map out your first few years as a homesteader. Then push yourself further. Share your experiences and help others develop skills that can help them become more self-sustaining. Homesteading is a lifestyle that brings joy and relief into your life while filling your days with tasks and hobbies that pay off day after day with outstanding physical and emotional rewards.

Resources

https://www.canr.msu.edu/news/7_benefits_of_eating_local_food
https://ag.purdue.edu/GMOs/Pages/GMOsandHealth.aspx
https://greatergood.berkeley.edu/article/item/how_modern_life_became_disconnected_from_nature
https://www.fsrmagazine.com/chain-restaurants/whats-americas-most-frequented-restaurant-chain
https://www.downsizinggovernment.org/agriculture/timeline
https://www.ncbi.nlm.nih.gov/books/NBK305168
https://scholarlykitchen.sspnet.org/2020/03/27/a-history-of-panic-buying/
https://www.cnn.com/2003/HEALTH/12/23/madcow.chronology.reut/
https://www.thespruce.com/top-tips-for-the-beginning-homesteader-3016686
http://www.quotehd.com/quotes/words/self%20sufficient
https://www.self-sufficient-farm-living.com
https://morningchores.com/starting-a-homestead/
https://www.agdaily.com/lifestyle/10-iconic-farming-quotes-history/
https://marketingartfully.com/5-goal-setting-systems/
https://www.workzone.com/blog/project-planning-quotes/
https://www.almanac.com/content/how-build-raised-garden-bed

https://www.thespruce.com/building-a-chicken-coop-3016589
https://www.motherearthnews.com/homesteading-and-livestock/raising-sheep-goats/raising-goats-backyard-farm-ze0z1204zsie
https://completelandscaping.com/much-space-need-fruit-trees/
https://www.blueberrycouncil.org/growing-blueberries/planting-blueberries/
https://www.countryfarm-lifestyles.com/Mini-Farms.html#.XuIkMi2z0Us
https://morningchores.com/assessing-and-planning-homestead/
https://www.primalsurvivor.net/1-acre-tiny-homestead-layouts/
http://www.thebeefsite.com/articles/2415/grazing-small-ruminants-with-cattle/
https://www.diynetwork.com/how-to/outdoors/gardening/manure-compost-
https://en.wikipedia.org/wiki/Cultivar
https://www.thespruce.com/cultivars-vs-varieties-how-do-they-differ-2132281
https://snaped.fns.usda.gov/seasonal-produce-guide
https://gilmour.com/cold-weather-crops
https://www.onegreenplanet.org/lifestyle/perennial-plants/
https://homeguides.sfgate.com/vegetables-grow-yearround-66602.html
https://nellinos.com/the-history-of-the-tomato-in-italy.html
https://www.tropicalpermaculture.com/tropical-vegetables.html
https://www.learningwithexperts.com/gardening/blog/10-flowers-to-grow-with-vegetables
https://www.westernexterminator.com/wasps/what-do-wasps-eat/
https://www.rspb.org.uk/birds-and-wildlife/wildlife-guides/other-garden-wildlife/insects-and-other-invertebrates/flies/hoverfly/
https://www.ufseeds.com/learning/garden-planting-guide/
https://books.google.com/books?id=r5hiDgAAQBAJ&pg=PA11&lpg=PA11&dq=Know+Your+Seed+Varieties+GMO+hybrid+heirloom+cell-fusion&source=bl&ots=nS5wcLmYd0&sig=ACfU3U1TSKgf23MSNmSLSRQaG9DcK3Q42w&hl=en&sa=X&ved=2ahUKEwjN8da2kITq

AhXCsZ4KHTa_DPAQ6AEwCXoECAoQAQ#v=onepage&q=Know%20Your%20Seed%20Varieties%20GMO%20hybrid%20heirloom%20cell-fusion&f=false

https://www.starmilling.com/what-to-do-with-a-broody-hen/https://www.cacklehatchery.com/cinnamon-queentm-chicken.html#product_tabs_breed_info

https://www.offthegridnews.com/how-to-2/best-homesteading-chickens/

https://www.thehappychickencoop.com/brahma-chicken/

https://morningchores.com/chicken-coop-plans/

https://www.construct101.com/chicken-coop-plans-design-2/

https://www.diyncrafts.com/34313/woodworking/20-free-diy-chicken-coop-plans-can-build-weekend

https://homesteading.com/how-to-build-a-chicken-coop/

https://104homestead.com/simple-living-kitchen-gadgets/

https://www.homestead.org/food/equip-your-homestead-kitchen-and-then-make-some-tasty-yogurt/

https://cheesemaking.com/collections/equipment

https://melissaknorris.com/how-to-organize-build-your-homestead-food-storage-kitchen/

https://apartmentprepper.com/how-to-preserve-meat-without-a-fridge-2/

https://www.healthline.com/nutrition/fermentation

http://fermentacap.com/how-long-do-fermented-foods-keep/

https://www.culturesforhealth.com/learn/water-kefir/water-kefir-frequently-asked-questions-faq/

https://www.liveeatlearn.com/homemade-milk-kefir/

https://traditionalcookingschool.com/food-preparation/how-long-does-kefir-last-aw060/

https://www.jerkyholic.com/how-long-does-beef-jerky-stay-good/

https://www.dummies.com/food-drink/canning/food-preservation-methods-canning-freezing-and-drying/

http://www.eatingwell.com/article/114109/how-to-pickle-anything-no-canning-necessary/
https://commonsensehome.com/home-food-preservation/#4_Freezing
https://commonsensehome.com/root-cellars-101/
https://www.rootwell.com/blogs/root-cellar
https://www.scientificamerican.com/article/experts-organic-milk-lasts-longer/
https://www.mediavillage.com/article/static-branding-vs-organic-branding-uwe-hook-mediabizbloggers/
https://definitions.uslegal.com/f/farmers-market/
http://www.flaginc.org/wp-content/uploads/2013/03/FarmersMarket.pdf
https://www.etsy.com/legal/policy/food-and-edible-items/239327355460
https://www.etsy.com/seller-handbook/article/recipe-for-success-7-tips-for-selling/22506251230
https://www.nolo.com/legal-encyclopedia/starting-home-based-food-business-california.html
https://www.theselc.org/cottage_food_law_summary
https://wwoof.net
https://wwoofusa.org/how-it-works/be-host
https://4-h.org
https://www.ffa.org
https://nifa.usda.gov/cooperative-extension-system
https://www.underatinroof.com/blog/2017/11/15/zmys9ruhc5wis7p5ntzo6idt75zr2i
https://www.grants.gov
https://www.usda.gov/topics/farming/grants-and-loans
https://www.nal.usda.gov/afsic
https://www.beginningfarmers.org
https://kidsgardening.org/gardening-basics-garden-maintenance-weeding-mulching-and-fertilizing/
https://homesteading.com/best-homesteading-tools/
https://morningchores.com/low-maintenance-homestead/

https://www.communitychickens.com/hens-stop-laying-zbw2002ztil/
https://www.farmsanctuary.org/wp-content/uploads/2012/06/Animal-Care-Goats.pdf
https://www.farmsanctuary.org/wp-content/uploads/2012/06/Animal-Care-Cattle.pdf
https://www.businessofapps.com/data/youtube-statistics/
https://learn.g2.com/how-much-do-youtubers-make
https://support.patreon.com/hc/en-us/articles/204606315-What-is-Patreon-
https://www.theselfsufficienthomeacre.com/2020/04/how-to-grow-food-in-small-spaces.html
https://www.motherearthnews.com/homesteading-and-livestock/homestead-working-dog-zmaz00aszgoe
https://homesteadsurvivalsite.com/best-dog-breeds-homesteaders/
https://www.thespruce.com/beginners-guide-to-beekeeping-3016857
https://www.motherearthnews.com/organic-gardening/aquaponic-gardening-growing-fish-vegetables-together
https://www.countryliving.com/gardening/garden-ideas/how-to/g1274/how-to-plant-a-vertical-garden/

Here's another book by Dion Rosser
that you might be interested in

Manufactured by Amazon.ca
Bolton, ON